WRITERS AND THEIR WORK

ISOBEL ARMSTRONG
General Editor

REVOLUTIONARY WOMEN WRITERS:
CHARLOTTE SMITH & HELEN MARIA WILLIAMS

REVOLUTIONARY WOMEN WRITERS:
CHARLOTTE SMITH & HELEN MARIA WILLIAMS

Angela Keane

© Copyright 2013 by Angela Keane

First published in 2013 by Northcote House Publishers Ltd, Horndon House, Horndon, Tavistock, Devon, PL19 9NQ, United Kingdom.
Tel: +44 (0) 1822 810066 Fax: +44 (0) 1822 810034.

All rights reserved. No part of this work may be reproduced or stored in an information retrieval system (other than short extracts for the purposes of review) without the express permission of the Publishers given in writing.

British Library Cataloguing-in-Publication Data
A catalogue record for this book is available from the British Library

ISBN 978-0-7463-1096-0 hardcover
ISBN 978-0-7463-0971-1 paperback

Typeset by PDQ Typesetting, Newcastle-under-Lyme
Printed and bound in the United Kingdom

Contents

Acknowledgements	vi
Biographical Outlines	vii
Abbreviations	xiii
Introduction	1
1 An Unfinished Work: Charlotte Smith's *Elegiac Sonnets*	7
2 Gossip and Politics in *Desmond*	21
3 Declarations of Independence in *The Old Manor House*	32
4 Double Vision and *The Emigrants*	44
5 Mourning Complete?: *Beachy Head*	59
6 The Ties That Bind: Williams' Poetry of the 1780s	69
7 Philosophical Passions: *Julia*	85
8 Revolution and Romance: *Letters from France*	99
9 Sublime Exile: *A Tour of Switzerland*	119
Afterword	131
Notes	133
Select Bibliography	145
Index	154

Acknowledgements

I would like to thank my colleagues in the School of English at the University of Sheffield, who have graciously tolerated the time it has taken me to complete this book, and provided the space for me to do so. Thanks to the scrupulous anonymous reader whose efforts have made my thoughts clearer and to my copy-editor Katie Ryde for her patience and attention to detail. For moral support (and childcare) I am grateful to Ruth Cross, Ros Fox, Sarah Gillibrand, Helene Herrington, Rebecca Howard, Sharon Keatley and Clare McGettigan. Thanks to my brothers and sisters who have shared with me too many sad losses in recent years, and who have propped me up when I've been flagging. For their unconditional love thanks to my children Sadie, Alfie and Iris Jones, whose respective arrivals considerably slowed the production of this book, but who have made the intervals between writing so rich. Finally, my biggest debt, for his patience, loyalty and love, is to Eddie Jones, who lives in hope that one day I'll write a bestseller. In the meantime, this book, and my love, are for him.

Biographical Outlines

CHARLOTTE SMITH

1749   On 4 May, Charlotte Turner is born to Anna Towers and Nicholas Turner, King Street, London; Nicholas also owns two estates, Stoke Place in Surrey and Bignor Park in Sussex.

1752   Anna Turner dies in childbirth; the three Turner children, Charlotte, Catherine and Nicholas Jnr., are left in the care of their maternal aunt, Lucy Towers, at Bignor Park while their father goes abroad.

1757   Nicholas Turner returns from abroad and moves his children to London; Charlotte goes to school in Kensington.

1761   Nicholas Turner sells Stoke Place to pay off gambling debts; Charlotte is taken out of school to be educated at home and introduced into London society.

1764   Nicholas Turner marries Henrietta Meriton, a wealthy heiress.

1765   In February, Charlotte marries Benjamin Smith, son of a West India merchant and Director of East India Company, Richard Smith; they move to an apartment over his warehouse in Cheapside, London.

1766   Some time in the spring, Charlotte gives birth to her first child, a son; there is no record of his name. Elizabeth Smith, Benjamin's mother, dies.

1767   In March, Richard Smith marries Charlotte's aunt Lucy; the Smiths' second son, Benjamin Berney, is born in April; the first child dies around this time; Richard Smith provides the family with a house in Southgate.

1768   A third son, William Towers, is born.

BIOGRAPHICAL OUTLINES

1769	In April a first daughter, Charlotte Mary, is born.
1770	Charlotte gives birth to a fourth son, Braithwaite.
1771	The Smiths move to a larger house in Tottenham; a sixth child, Nicholas Hankey, arrives.
1773	Charlotte gives birth to her sixth son, Charles Dyer.
1774	Anna Augusta, the Smiths' eighth child, is born; the family moves to Lys Farm in Hampshire.
1776	A third daughter, Lucy Eleanor, is born; in October, Richard Smith dies, leaving an estate of £36,000 and a complex will.
1777	In June, the Smiths' eldest child, Benjamin Berney, dies, aged 11; in October, Charlotte gives birth to another son, Lionel.
1782	A fourth daughter is born in April.
1783	In December, Benjamin Smith is sent to King's Bench Prison for seven months for embezzlement of his father's trust fund; Lys Farm is sold. The Smiths' children are sent to live with Charlotte's brother while she spends time with Benjamin in prison and attempts to have him released.
1784	James Dodsley offer to publish *Elegiac Sonnets* with no advance for Charlotte; in desperation to raise money to pay Benjamin's debts she agrees. In June, the poems are published as *Elegiac Sonnets and other Essays*, by Charlotte Smith of Bignor Park, Sussex. In July, Benjamin Smith exchanges executorship of his father's trust with his creditors Dyer and Robinson in return for his release from prison. In July 1784, Benjamin takes up residence in Dieppe. In October, Charlotte and the children join Benjamin in a dilapidated chateau in Normandy.
1785	In February, Charlotte gives birth to her eighth son George in Normandy. In the spring, Charlotte and the ten surviving children return to England; Charlotte rents a house in Woolbeding, Sussex.
1786	In June, Charlotte's 16-year-old son Braithwaite dies after a short illness. In September, Cadell publish her two-volume translation of Prévost's *Manon Lescaut*. It is received with great controversy and Smith withdraws it from publication.
1787	Cadell publish *The Romance of Real Life* based on stories in Gayot de Pivatol's *Les Causes Célèbres*; the family move to

	Wyke, Surrey; in April, Charlotte separates from Benjamin Smith.
1788	Cadell publish *Emmeline, the Orphan of the Castle*.
1789	Cadell publish *Ethelinde, or the Recluse of the Lake*; Smith and her children move to Brighton.
1791	Cadell publish *Celestina. A novel*.
1792	Robinson publish *Desmond. A novel*.
1793	Joseph Bell publishes *The Old Manor House* in March. Cadell publish *The Emigrants, a poem, in two books*. In August the family move to Storrington in Sussex.
1794	Bell publishes *The Wanderings of Warwick*; Smith moves to Bath with her daughter Harriet. In August, Cadell and Davies publish *The Banished Man*.
1795	Smith's beloved daughter Anna Augusta dies in April; Sampson Law publish *Montalbert. A novel*. Cadell and Davies publish *Rural Walks: in dialogues: intended for the use of young persons*.
1796	Charlotte moves to Weymouth; in August, Cadell and Davies publish *Rambles Farther. A Continuation of Rural Walks* and Low publishes *Marchmont. A novel*.
1797	Cadell and Davies publish *Elegiac Sonnets*, Volume 2.
1798	In June, Low publishes *Minor Morals* and, in June, Cadell and Davies publish *The Young Philosopher*; Charlotte moves to London.
1800	Low publishes *The Letters of a Solitary Wanderer*, Volumes 1–3.
1801	Charlotte's son, Charles, dies aged 28. Charlotte moves to Frant.
1802	Longman publish *The Letters of a Solitary Wanderer*, Volumes 4–5.
1803	Charlotte runs out of money; moves to Elsted in Susssex.
1804	Joseph Johnson publishes *Conversations introducing Poetry... For the use of children and young persons*.
1805	Charlotte moves to Tilford near Farnham, Surrey.
1806	In February, Benjamin Smith dies in debtor's prison in Berwick-upon-Tweed; Charlotte's marriage settlements are freed up for her children. In September, Charlotte's youngest son George dies. In October, Charlotte Smith dies at Tilford. She is buried at Stoke Church, near Guildford.

1807	Joseph Johnson publishes *Beachy Head, Fables, and Other Poems*.
1813	In April, Richard Smith's estate is finally settled.

HELEN MARIA WILLIAMS

1761	Helen Maria Williams is born in London on 17 June to Helen Hay and Charles Williams. The Williamses were a propertied family, and Charles was an army officer, who had served as the Secretary for Minorca. Helen and Charles had one other daughter, Cecilia, believed to be older than Helen Maria. Charles had another daughter, Persis, from a previous marriage.
1762	In December, Charles Williams dies, leaving an estate that would provide a substantial living for his family.
c.1763	The Williamses move to Berwick-upon-Tweed. The girls are raised in the Presbyterian tradition.
1781	The family moves back to London.
1782	Under the mentorship of Andrew Kippis, a Presbyterian minister, prominent dissenter, and contributor to a range of periodicals, HMW has her first poem, the medieval ballad *Edwin and Eltruda*, published by Cadell. Kippis introduces her to his literary circle.
1783	*Ode on the Peace*, inspired by the end of the American war, is published by Cadell.
1784	Cadell publish HMW's six-canto epyllion, *Peru*.
1786	HMW's two-volume collection, *Poems*, is published by Cadell. The first edition has around 1,500 subscribers.
1788	HMW's *A Poem on the Bill Lately Passed for Regulating the Slave Trade*, published by Cadell, is part of a broader campaign for Abolition in the late 1780s. 'The Morai. An Ode', on Captain James Cook's exploration of Tahiti, is published in an appendix to Kippis's biography of Cook.
1790	In March, HMW's first, and only, novel, *Julia*, is published by Cadell. In July, HMW joins her sister and mother in France, where they stay with their friends, Monsieur and Madame du Fossé. She returns to England in September. In November, the first volume of *Letters from France*, entitled *Letters Written in France, in the*

	Summer 1790, appears, published by Cadell.
1791	HMW announces her imminent return to France, in a poem published by Cadell, entitled *A Farewell, for Two Years, to England*. In August, she travels to France.
1792	The second volume of *Letters from France* appears. HMW returns to England in June, and travels back to France in August. HMW meets the dissenter and businessman, John Hurford Stone, in France. He is still married at this time.
1793	*Letters from France*, volumes 3 and 4, appear. From October to December, HMW and her family are imprisoned in the Luxembourg prison and the convent of Les Anglaises.
1794	Stone and his wife divorce. In June, Stone and Williams leave Paris for Switzerland, returning in December. Stone joins the Williams household.
1795	Volumes 1-3 of the second series of *Letters from France* appear. HMW's translation of Bernadin de Saint-Pierre's *Paul and Virginia* is published by Longman
1796	Volume 4 of *Letters from France*, second series, is published. 'On the death of the Rev. Dr. Kippis' is published in *Gentleman's Magazine*.
1798	HMW's sister, Cecilia, dies, leaving two small sons in the care of HMW and her mother. *A Tour in Switzerland* is published by Robinson.
1801	*Sketches of the State of Manners and Opinions in the French Republic* is published by Robinson. 'Ode to Peace' appears in the *Morning Chronicle* on 17 November. The poem incurs Napoleon's anger and prompts a one-day imprisonment for HMW.
1803	HMW edits *The Political and Confidential Correspondence of Lewis the Sixteenth* in 3 volumes, published by Robinson, and Napoleon tries to suppress it.
1809	HMW writes *Verses addressed by HMW to Her Two Nephews on Saint Helen's Day*, published in Paris.
1812	In April, HMW's mother dies.
1814	HMW translates Alexander von Humboldt's *Researches concerning... Inhabitants of America and Personal Narrative of Travels to the New Continent*, which are published by Longman. *Personal Narrative* was published in seven volumes between 1814 and 1829.

1815	After the defeat of Napoleon HMW resumes her historical and political writing, with *A Narrative of Events Which Have Taken Place in France from the Landing of Napoleon Bonaparte to the Restoration of Louis XVIII*, which is published by Murray of London.
1816	HMW comes to the defence of Protestants in the south of France, who were subjected to violent persecution after Waterloo, in her pamphlet, *On the late Persecution of the Protestants*, published in London by Underwood.
1817	HMW translates *The Leper of the City of Aoste*, by Xavier de Maistre, published in London by George Cowie. HMW and Stone are naturalized as French citizens.
1818	In May, John Hurford Stone dies. HMW has his tombstone engraved with the words 'enlightened champion of Religion and Liberty. Last Tribute to a Long Friendship. HMW'.
1819	*Letters on the Events Which have Passed in France Since the Restoration in 1815* is published in London, by Baldwin. HMW writes *The Charter, Lines Addressed by Helen Maria Williams, to her Nephew Athanase C. Coquerel, on His Wedding Day*, which is published in Paris.
1823	HMW's *Poems on Various Subjects* is published by Whittaker of London. HMW moves to Amsterdam. In December, Persis Williams dies.
1827	HMW returns to Paris. Her *Souvenirs de la révolution française* is published in Paris, translated from English by her nephew, Charles Coquerel. On 15 December, aged 66, HMW dies.

Abbreviations

AT	*An American Tale* in *Poems, 1786*, vol. 1, 13–14.
BH	*Beachy Head* in Curran, 213–47.
Curran	*The Poems of Charlotte Smith*, ed. by Stuart Curran (Oxford: Oxford University Press, 1993).
D	Charlotte Smith, *Desmond*, ed. by Antje Blank and Janet Todd (Ontario: Broadview Press, 2001).
EE	*Edwin and Eltruda: A Legendary Tale* in *Poems, 1786*, vol. 1, 61–100.
FE	*A Farewell, for Two Years, to England* in *LFF*, vol. 1, 207–12
Julia	Helen Maria Williams, *Julia, A Novel*, 2 vols (London: Cadell, 1790).
LFF, 1	Helen Marian Williams, *Letters written in France, in the Summer 1790, to a Friend in England*, ed. by Neil Fraistat and Susan S. Lanser ([1790]; Ontario: Broadview Press, 2001).
LFF, 2–8	Helen Maria Williams, *Letters From France*, ed. by Janet Todd, 8 vols (Delmar, New York: Scholars Facsimilies and Reprints, 1975).
OP	*An Ode on the Peace*, in *Poems, 1786*, vol. 1, 35–60.
Peru	*Peru*, in *Poems, 1786*, vol. 2, 45–178.
Poems 1786	Helen Maria Williams, *Poems, 1786*, 2 vols (Oxford: Woodstock Books, 1994).
Poems VS	Helen Maria Williams, *Poems on Various Subjects. With Introductory Remarks on the Present State of Science and Literature in France* (London: Whittaker, 1823).
RST	Helen Maria Williams, *A Poem on the Bill Lately Passed for Regulating the Slave Trade* (London: Cadell, 1788).
Stanton	*The Collected Letters of Charlotte Smith*, ed. by Judith Phillips Stanton (Bloomington and Indianapolis: Indiana University Press, 2003).

TE	*The Emigrants* in Curran, 135–63.
TOMH	Charlotte Smith, *The Old Manor House*, ed. by Jacqueline M. Labbe (Ontario: Broadview Press, 2002).
TS	Helen Maria Williams, *A Tour of Switzerland; or, A View of the Prsent State of the Governments and Manners of those Cantons; with Comparative Sketches of the Present State of Paris*, 2 vols (London: Robinson, 1798).

Note on the Choice of Texts

I have largely selected the most discussed and readily accessible of Smith's and Williams' texts. Where available, I have used paperback editions rather than, in the case of Smith, the *Collected Works*, again for reasons of accessibility.

Introduction

In the time between the promise that I would write this book and its delivery its subjects have outgrown the format. Even five years ago it seemed reasonable to devote only a single volume of this series to Helen Maria Williams and Charlotte Smith, not because their achievements in their lifetime were minor, but because much of their work was still not readily accessible and critical debate on the two was fairly localized. Charlotte Smith, in particular, now seems constrained by the half-volume I have dedicated to her. There is now a collected *Works of Charlotte Smith* from Pickering and Chatto, Judith Stanton's *Collected Letters*, as well as Stuart Curran's Oxford edition of her *Poems*, numerous Broadview editions of her novels and a critical biography.[1] Critical debate has moved well beyond arguing for her inclusion in the Romantic canon. Smith's critics now have enough to say to argue amongst themselves. That would have pleased the querulous Smith. Williams' status is slighter and scholarly editions of her work are harder to come by, but on-line collections, a recent biography and a growing body of criticism mean that her work is also easier to teach, talk about and take for granted.

In the 1790s, when both women were at the peak of their critical reputations, they were known to each other and often cited together. Smith provided the young William Wordsworth with a letter of introduction to Williams when he visited Orléans in 1791, but Williams had already left for Paris when he arrived. On 18 November 1792, when a group of British exiles living in Paris gathered to celebrate the defeat of the Austrian army by the French, they raised a toast 'to the Women of Great Britain, particularly those who have distinguished themselves by their writings in favour of the French Revolution, Mrs Smith

1

and Miss H. M. Williams'.[2] Smith had recently written her pro-revolutionary novel *Desmond* and Williams was living in Paris and had completed several volumes of her eight-volume *Letters from France*. On the other side of the Channel, and on the other side of revolutionary feeling, Smith and Williams were to be joined together more pejoratively in Richard Polwhele's misogynist tirade *The Unsex'd Females*.[3] The poem tore into the women who had come to prominence through art and literature at the end of the eighteenth century. Smith and Williams are mentioned as two amongst many who gave up properly feminine forms of expression in pursuit of 'the Rights of womankind' (a play on the title of Wollstonecraft's polemic and a poem by Anna Laetitia Barbauld):

> Charming SMITH resign'd her power to please,
> Poetic feeling and poetic ease;
> And HELEN, fir'd by Freedom, bade adieu
> To all the broken visions of Peru; (ll.95–8)

Polwhele refers here to Smith's and Williams' apparently more acceptable poetry of the 1780s, Smith's *Elegiac Sonnets* and Williams' mini-epic, *Peru*. Both women began their careers as poets, and moved in the 1790s to prose, predominantly fiction by Smith and historical and political letters for Williams, although both produced more poetry later in their careers.

Smith's sympathetic and hostile reviewers invariably focus on the self-representation and melancholy that marks her work. Smith's difficult downwardly mobile life, dogged by an acrimonious separation from the father of her twelve children (some of whom died in infancy) and the pursuit of their rightful legacy, is glimpsed in prefaces, notes and asides throughout her work. In the preface to the sixth edition of the *Sonnets*, Smith invites readers to find her life in her works, claiming the melancholy of the poems as her own: 'I wrote mournfully because I was unhappy'.[4] Readers of her blank-verse poem, *The Emigrants*, tire of her tendency to insert her own history into her writing. The *European Magazine*'s anonymous respondent to *The Emigrants* writes, impatiently, that 'The whole Poem may be considered as a soliloquy pronounced by the authoress'.[5] The *Critical Review* is even less tolerant, finding that Smith 'begins and ends the piece' and any pity we feel for the French emigrants is 'lessened by their being brought into parallel with the inconveniences of a narrow income'.[6] After her death, Walter Scott can find some sympathy for the downbeat character of Smith's writing, although he sees no gap between authorial and textual woes. 'Every one', he writes, 'must regret that the tone of melancholy which pervades Mrs Smith's compositions, was derived too surely from the circumstances and feelings of the amiable Authoress.'[7]

Smith's tendency to self-revelation has been redeemed and complicated by recent readers; critics who, in Theresa Kelly's words, have moved 'rather quickly from the textual recovery of a Romantic woman poet who mourned her marginal, inadequate relation to the male tradition... to the recognition that Smith capably staged a Romantic poetic persona for whom loss and recovery and diffusion are the rhetorical work at hand and the labor [sic] of poetic speech'.[8] Modern criticism, that is, has recovered Smith's work and made us ask questions about the gap between the writer and that work, and the proximity between the autobiographical unhappiness and its textual performance. The purpose of Smith's work is not just to represent misery but to enact and recoup the emotional and material losses of her life.

In the work of Helen Maria Williams there is an explicit and polite distance between authorial subject and textual performance, a distance that makes her a less likely candidate than Smith for inclusion in the Romantic canon. Even though the work for which she is most famous, *Letters from France*, is a first-person account of her own experiences in Paris, there is little authorial reflection on the intimate aspects of her life: the growing relationship between Williams and British businessman John Hurford Stone; the financial and domestic circumstances in which she lived with her sisters and mother; her responses to personal grief and illness. Although this is a self-consciously 'emotional account' of the revolutionary years, an affair of 'the imagination, the understanding and the heart', the emotional response is recorded according to the codes of eighteenth-century sentimentalism.[9] Contemporary reviewers recognize and appreciate the artifice. They use terms like 'unaffected' and 'sincere' but they also write of the 'effusion of a young and fervid imagination', the 'sprightly and entertaining' character of the letters, connoting the *Letters'* self-conscious, constructed character.[10] Early reviewers seem pleased by Williams' feminine affability. She has, according to the *Analytical*'s reviewer, the knack of 'chatting on paper', a sort of salon sociability, and an ability to bring the topic of the day to life without testing the patience or compromising the propriety of the reader.[11] Even so, *The General Magazine* finds in the 'familiarity' of epistolary composition a vivacity that borders on the improper: 'In a young writer, and especially a female one, the saucy little pronoun *I* seldom makes its appearance with a good grace'.[12] As Williams' political views began to be taken more seriously and as hostility to French revolutionary politics grew in England, critical condescension turned to open condemnation. Polwhele's *The Unsex'd Females* was followed by other satirical attacks. Kirkpatrick Sharpe's 'The Vision of Liberty' and George Canning's 'The New Morality' were savage in their caricatures of Williams and other so-called 'Jacobins' (revolutionary sympathisers). In 'The New Morality', Williams is characterized with Paine, Godwin and Holcroft ('All creeping creatures, venoumous and low') as a devotee of the 'theophilanthropist' Lepaux.[13] In fact, in Williams' *Tour in Switzerland*, she indicts the 'rage' for theophilanthropy as just another revolutionary fashion.[14] In the Spenserian imitation, 'The Vision of Liberty', Williams is lechery in a procession of the Seven Deadly Sins (the others represented by Paine, Wollstonecraft, Godwin and other 'radicals'):

> Then came Maria Helen Williams Stone,
> Sitting upon a goat with bearded chin;
> And she hath written volumes many a one;
> Better the idle jade had learned to spin.[15]

Better, that is, that she had not taken up with Stone nor written *Letters from France* and had been a 'spinster' instead of a 'jade', an improper woman.

The presumption of sexual impropriety in radical women was commonplace. After all, a woman's sexual character was, in the eighteenth century, the only character she had. The association between revolutionary politics and sexual impropriety was made most strongly in relation to Williams in Laetitia Matilda Hawkins' *Letters on the Female Mind*, addressed particularly to the author of *Letters from France*.[16] Hawkins makes use of the longstanding antipathy of the British patriot to the degenerate French, to argue that 'susceptible' women like Williams (i.e. women who are both too masculine and too highly sexed) have succumbed to the seductions of revolutionary philosophy, or the 'French disease' as counter-revolutionaries dubbed it, sealing the connection between sexual and political 'infection'.[17]

Williams was not only indicted for her revolutionary sympathies. Her presumption to write 'history' was another cause for critique. Her nineteenth-century entry in the *Dictionary of National Biography* refers to her accounts of historical events as impressions 'frequently formed on very imperfect, one-sided, and garbled information, travestied by the enthusiasm of a clever, badly educated woman and uttered with the cocksureness of ignorance'. M. Ray Adams, writing in the late 1930s, calls Williams a 'political romanticist' and 'flighty; so embarrassed is she by the multitude of things to be put down that she sometimes cannot follow an exposition through'.[18] Recent critics have taken a more sympathetic view of Williams' writing style and her understanding of historical representation, exploring her use of fictional tropes and a particularly feminine approach to the recording of public events.[19]

The combination of Charlotte Smith's 'impolite' assaults upon the sensibilities of her readers, imploring their patronage and their understanding in her *Sonnets* and her fiction, and the intricate meditations on subjective knowledge and perspective in *The Emigrants* and *Beachy Head* have, arguably, earned her a place in an expanded Romantic canon. Williams does not inscribe herself in her texts in the same way. The subject at the centre of her texts is a feeling, empathetic woman of sensibility but she does not reflect on and revise the controlling consciousness in the way that Smith's subject often does. At the end of her writing career, and near the end of her life, Williams asks for the indulgence of a generation of readers to whom, she suspects, her sensibilities and writing style are already out of date. 'My literary patrons belonged to "the days of other years,"' she writes in the preface to her 1823 volume of poetry, 'when a ray of favour sometimes fell on my early essays in verse'.[20] Williams senses an emerging fashion – Romanticism? – with which she is at odds. Smith and Williams, then, who write at the same historical moment, and emerge from a similar social and literary milieu, end their careers looking in two different directions. Smith, who died some twenty years before Williams, looks towards and perhaps in *Beachy Head* beyond Romanticism. Williams stays firmly behind it, clinging on to the aesthetics and mores of a late eighteenth-century liberal cosmopolitanism that, by her death in the late 1820s, had been eclipsed in Britain by more inward-looking poetics and a more nationalistic sense of culture.

The inclusion of these two writers in a single volume can be vindicated in part by the light they shed on the relationship of women writers to Romanticism. Smith's work asks us to expand the Romantic canon, to do as Wordsworth expected we would not, and recognize the formal contribution of a woman 'to whom English verse is under greater obligations than are likely to be either acknowledged or remembered'.[21] Williams' more opaque and remote collection of poetry, fiction and letters, ask us to see what was going on at the turn of the nineteenth century outside of Romanticism, and to pay our dues to a radical whose politics did not give way to reaction despite the provocation of the Terror, the rise and fall of Napoleon or the personal attacks on her character. A moment of self-defence in the *Souvenirs* is fitting testimony to this aspect of Williams' career:

> I...have always been on the side of the oppressed...It is not true that I have preached, turn by turn, as others say, the symbols of the terror, the imperial eagle and the white flag. I believe I have lived through the revolution with more constancy. Far from humbly acknowledging myself guilty of such a fault, I dare, on the contrary, reclaim a part of the merit belonging to the friends of liberty, for having so long defended the cause.[22]

In the course of her writing career Williams does qualify and reign-in her early enthusiasms for revolutionary politics but she is never as sceptical or satirical as Smith. There is a rudeness at the heart of Smith's discourse, a desire to intrude upon the reader that appeals perhaps more to a modern audience than to her contemporaries and that is more compelling than Williams' paradoxically polite radicalism. These two variously 'improper' women, then, have different but equally intriguing stories to tell us about political and literary expression at the turn of the nineteenth century.

1

An Unfinished Work: Charlotte Smith's *Elegiac Sonnets*

By the time Charlotte Smith's first publication, her *Elegiac Sonnets*, appeared in June 1784, she was the mother of nine surviving children and of two who had already died. She had spent much of the previous year negotiating her husband's release from King's Bench, a debtor's prison.[1] When this was finally secured, Smith and the children followed Benjamin Smith to Normandy, where, in straitened circumstances, Charlotte Smith gave birth to another son in February 1785. By then the second edition of the *Sonnets* had been published and the collection was receiving positive reviews back in England. Although she had received no advance from her publisher Dodsley, Smith was set to make some profit from the collection, which eventually went into ten editions. In 1784, any profit would have helped to relieve the burden of debt she carried courtesy of her husband Benjamin.

Such biographical detail might seem extraneous to the critical understanding of Charlotte Smith's sonnets. To allude to her status as a mother might seem to offer not only a biographical but also a 'biological' context for her poetic production, as though the poems were peculiarly linked to her female body. Smith's sonnets do inhabit a self-consciously biographical domain, one that Smith insists we understand in the prefaces to the many editions of the *Sonnets*. But the poems provide us with mediated access to the poet – mediated by the generic history of the sonnet, by the eighteenth-century culture of melancholy and by the emerging conditions of authorship.

SONNET REVIVAL

Smith's contemporaries William Wordsworth and Samuel Taylor Coleridge credited her for the revival of popular and critical interest in the sonnet. Smith and William Lisle Bowles are cited as the inspirations for Coleridge's own experiments with the sonnet form, and for hundreds of less well-known poets who turned sonneteer at the end of the eighteenth century. The sonnet had been popular amongst English writers of the early modern period, who took inspiration from the fourteenth-century Italian poet, Petrarch, and his musings on the pains of love, which were neatly organized into eight and six line sections (the octave and the sestet) and regular rhyme schemes that seemed to impose order on the chaos of amorous attraction. The English variants of the sonnet, known as the Shakespearian and Spenserian forms after their most celebrated practitioners, provided a new four-part structure (three quatrains and a couplet) each part with a self-contained rhyme scheme. John Donne provided a new twist on the sonnet's content when he refigured the secular love of the Petrarchan tradition as divine love and John Milton coined the political sonnet in the seventeenth century.

The sonnet was dormant in the early part of the eighteenth century, when 'major' poets like Pope, Dryden and Swift dispensed with the fourteen-line form and its apparent lyricism, in favour of often didactic and satiric content in essays (in verse and prose), epistles, mock-epics and social comedies or comedies of manners. Stuart Curran sees this rejection of the sonnet form by these urbane poets as 'a symptom of the cultural distance the eighteenth century imposed between itself and the Elizabethans, who were commonly understood to have been barbaric'.[2] Artists of the late eighteenth century on the other hand evidently revelled in barbarism as they looked back even further than the Elizabethans for their inspiration and embraced medieval architecture, ancient romances, and all things that stirred sensation rather than tickled the intellect. The neglected sonnet form was washed up on this wave of medievalism, and the new sonneteers were infected by the morbid aesthetic of Gothic culture. So, in the work of Bowles and Smith, sonnets that explore the agonies of amorous devotion are accompanied by evocations of more generalized melancholy, grief and the condition of loss.

The provenance of Smith's interest in the sonnet probably lies in her reading of Shakespeare, although amongst the eighty-four *Elegiac Sonnets* there are imitations of Petrarch and allusions to other poets associated with the form, including Milton and Sidney. The literary influences on display in the *Sonnets* extend beyond other sonneteers, however. There are quotations from Pope, Thomson and Shakespeare; allusions to William Mason, Edward Young, William Hayley, Thomas Otway, William Collins, John Sargent, Ann Yearsley, Thomas Chatterton and Thomas Gray.[3] If there is no surviving catalogue of Smith's personal library, at least these are the obvious signs of her poetic taste.[4] It is a taste marked – predominantly – by sorrow. In the preface to the sixth edition of the first volume of *Elegiac Sonnets*, Smith is eager to let us know that the sorrows of which she has written for the past nine years are hers, that they are private and that they are unrelenting:

> [when] I first struck the chords of the melancholy lyre, its notes were never intended for the public ear! It was unaffected sorrows drew them forth: I wrote mournfully because I was unhappy – And I have unfortunately no reason yet, though nine years have since elapsed, to *change my tone*. (Curran, 5)

By 1790 Smith had yet no reason to change her tone, because she was still waiting for her children's inheritance from their paternal grandfather, who died in 1776, to be made available.[5] She was still waiting for financial relief until her death. Smith never shied away from publicizing her impecunious position and there were other sorrows to which she drew the public's attention. Like many people of that time, Smith experienced much personal grief. When she was three her mother died and she survived six of her twelve children. Her social status sustained a number of attacks. Born into a genteel family from Sussex, her ill-advised marriage to Benjamin Smith and the labyrinth of her children's inheritance case meant that Smith spent most of her life fending off debt. For Smith, writing was less a respectable way of life than a means of survival.

Despite the compelling narrative force of Smith's financial and emotional problems and the fact that Smith repeatedly foregrounds them in the prefaces to her work, it is a mistake to take Smith at her word and to make a direct identification between the biographical Smith and the speakers of her sonnets.[6] Jacqueline Labbe has demonstrated this point to great effect in her study of Smith's poetry. Labbe draws her terminology from recent theories about the performative and flexible – rather than natural and stable – character of gendered identity, and argues that 'far from offering a sustained picture of personal sorrow, the *Sonnets* are a compendium of identities and voices, linked by an "I" who changes costume with ease, and stage-managed and directed by Smith'.[7] Labbe grounds her persuasive argument about the artifice in Smith's sonnets in modern theories of gender identity. However, another way to complicate the picture of the *Sonnets* as the unmediated expressions of woe of an unhappy woman is to consider them as part of an eighteenth-century literary tradition, which invites us to look at the artifice of the performance rather than the integrity of the expression. Perhaps it is not the sonnet tradition, but a tradition which has generic links with Smith's *Sonnets* (that is, which shares the same subject matter and themes) that provides the most suggestive genealogy and that helps us to come to terms with the tone and mood of Smith's poetry: the elegiac tradition.

ELEGY

Although the elegy in the strict sense is a lament for the death of a particular individual, late eighteenth-century poems like Thomas Gray's 'Elegy Written in a Country Churchyard' (1751) and Edward Young's *Night Thoughts* (1745) are more generalized responses to transience and loss experienced by speakers whose primary characteristics are powerlessness, marginality and impoverishment.[8] Gray's speaker is a solitary, nocturnal figure who contemplates the 'rude forefathers' of the hamlet served by the church and its graveyard, each asleep in his 'narrow cell'. In his own imagined epitaph, he is 'A youth to fortune and fame unknown' marked by 'Melancholy...for her own' (ll.118–20); a figure known to the locals for his 'listless' recumbence by the brook, for his 'muttering' of 'wayward fancies' and his 'drooping' posture. Young's speaker wakes from 'disturbed repose', only to reflect 'how happy they who wake no more!' (ll.6–7). Gray's and Young's speakers are eighteenth-century men of sensibility, characterized by mood, not by action or status. The culture of sensibility assumed that the powerless, the marginal, the impoverished, and the unhappy were fit subjects for art. In sentimental literature it was often the artist, or the artist's fictional representative in the text, who felt most keenly the want of power and financial security. This context, in Loraine Fletcher's words, provides Charlotte Smith with 'the confidence to assume that her depression, economic vulnerability and fears for her children are no improper subjects for one of the most historically privileged genres', the sonnet.[9]

While Gray's and Young's speakers are at least identifiable as melancholic young men, it is difficult to identify many of Smith's speakers by age or gender. They are the wronged friend, the night-time wanderer, the broken-hearted, the grief-stricken. Some poems *are* written in the voice of identifiable characters. Sonnets 21 to 25 are written in the voice of Goethe's sentimental hero Werther and readers familiar with Smith's other work would recognize sonnets which first appeared in her novels, penned by male and female characters.[10] Often the sonnets address a person, object, place, time or concept (to a friend, the nightingale, the South Downs, the spring, hope). In such poems a brief meditation on the addressee precedes a reflection on the speaker's emotional despair. Smith's speakers are united by a powerlessness that produces a profound sense of isolation, of distance from other subjects in the poems and of personal dislocation or uncertainty about their own identity. They are like Gray's youth, who can identify with neither the peasant nor the politician, and can conjure an image of himself seen from the outside, lounging 'listless' under a tree, babbling 'crazed with care' and finally 'borne' through the 'church-way path' after his death. Similarly, Smith's speakers feel no connection with the various pastoral figures who people their worlds: the 'blest... shepherd' (Sonnet 9); the 'hind' who gives his hours to 'wholesome labour' (Sonnet 31); the Laplander in winter who looks forward to the return of spring (Sonnet 53); the sleeping woodman (Sonnet 54); he who wanders in the woods, reposes on the banks or sits on the rocks (Sonnet 81). Smith evokes a sense of alienation that jars with the pastoral settings of many of her poems, settings that traditionally evoke unity and wholeness. The disunity generated by a subject at odds with their environment is often reinforced at the level of form. Sonnet 9, 'Blest is yon shepherd', for instance, gives us a Petrarchan octave and sestet, but the first 4 lines, describing the recumbent shepherd, have a Shakespearian or Spenserian rhyme scheme (ab ab):

> Blest is yon shepherd, on the turf reclined,
> Who on the varied clouds which float above
> Lies idly gazing – while his vacant mind
> Pours out some tale antique of rural love!
>
> (Curran, Sonnet 9, ll.1–4)

Thereafter the rhyme breaks down completely (bccdcdefef) as the speaker reflects on the deception of friends from which the shepherd has been protected:

> Ah! *he* has never felt the pangs that move
> Th'indignant spirit, when with selfish pride,
> Friends, on whose faith the trusting heart rely'd,
> Unkindly shun th'imploring eye of woe!
> The ills they ought to soothe, with taunts deride,
> And laugh at tears themselves have forced to flow.
> Nor *his* rude bosom those fine feelings melt,
> Children of Sentiment and Knowledge born,
> Thro' whom each shaft with cruel force is felt,
> Empoison'd by deceit – or barb'd with scorn.
>
> (Curran, Sonnet 9, ll.5–14)

The distance in this and other sonnets between speaker and object is created by the speaker's sensitivity to, and the object's supposed immunity from, suffering. Indeed, one of the characteristics of Smith's labourers is their easy repose (the woodman of Sonnet 54 is sleeping, not chopping). From the 'blest shepherd' of Sonnet 9 we move to the 'blest... hind':

> who from his bed of flock
> Starts – when the birds of morn their summons give,
> And waken'd by the lark – 'the shepherd's clock,'
> Lives but to labour – labouring but to live.
>
> (Curran, Sonnet 57, ll.5–8)

The suggestion in this poem is that the shepherd's happiness in his work is produced by an absence of self-reflection. Other reposing figures in the sonnets seem not to be labourers of any kind, but enjoy a 'refined retirement' and a life of rural leisure (see Sonnet 81, for instance). It might strike us as peculiar that in these poems there are very few hints of the rural impoverishment that many of her contemporaries, such as Ann Yearsley, Robert Burns and predecessors like Stephen Duck, Mary Collier and Oliver Goldsmith – all writers she admired – documented in verse. It is too simplistic, however, to criticize Smith for idealizing rural life. 'Rustic' figures, like the shepherd in this sonnet, are *so* idealized that they need to be understood as projections of the speaker's own desires, of his/her pastoral fantasy of an independent life. Thus in Sonnet 57, 'To Dependence', the happy labours of the shepherd in the octave are, in the sestet, contrasted with the art of the 'sycophant' (Curran, Sonnet 57, 9): the artist who is in thrall to a patron.[11] On the other occasion that Smith considers patronage, Sonnet 82, 'To the shade of Burns', the beneficiary of patronage is a 'parasite' whose 'abject chime' (Curran, Sonnet 82, l.8) has been privileged over the 'wild notes' of the Scottish poet who was 'fired with a love of freedom' (Curran, Sonnet 82, l.6).

While Smith had literary associates who offered support and introductions to publishers, she did not have a patron to underwrite her publications financially.[12] Some editions of her sonnets were published by subscription and others, like her novels, were published for the open market, some with advances, others without. Smith's stormy relationship with her publishers is notorious. Her letters include many embattled missives to Dodsley, Cadell and Davies and Robinson and her novel *The Banished Man* (1795) includes a barely disguised self-portrait in the shape of Charlotte Denzil, a female author at war with her demanding and unsympathetic publishers.[13] With neither financial independence nor the protection of patronage, Smith's publishers were not only her paymasters but also her creditors, as her spending often anticipated profits from the sales of her work. Such financial dependence did not sit lightly on Smith's shoulders, and informed the way in which she characterized the labour of writing. Her letters to publishers are simultaneously a catalogue of disruptions and obstructions to the writing process (the demands of her family; the absence of source material; the labyrinthine pursuit of her children's inheritance; the importunity of her husband) and of the imperative to write. To use Marxist terminology, writing is for Smith an alienated labour or a process of reification; that is, she writes knowing that the writing is not the property of the author but that it is a 'product', an object that is consumed. The signs of the relationship between the writing and the author – of the human process of writing – are erased at the point of consumption. The sorrows that she reiterates in her sonnets are not simply Smith's autobiographical sorrows but the sorrows of the modern author. The modern author, exemplified by Smith's sonneteer is, I want to argue, culturally if not constitutionally melancholic.

MELANCHOLY

As the examples of her predecessors Gray and Young suggest, Charlotte Smith did not invent the literature of melancholy but, for a while, she certainly cornered the market in it. Melancholy, once thought to be physiologically based, the 'condition of having too much "black bile"' was, by the late eighteenth century, understood more as a kind of temperament, associated with 'sadness and depression of spirits', a habitual 'condition of gloom or dejection', or, in a lighter sense 'a tender or pensive sadness' (*OED*). As a condition long associated with the sedentary, ruminating classes, it is a subject of which that most sedentary and ruminating class – writers – have first-hand experience. Melancholy is thus 'anatomized', eulogized, apostrophized, personified and vilified throughout literary history. Its mid to late eighteenth-century manifestation in the literature of sensibility is a variation on a long-standing theme. Eighteenth-century commentaries on the increasing visibility of melancholia often attributed this wave to the response of 'sensitive', introverted individuals – particularly men – to a period of economic expansion and political 'outwardness', the rise of consumerism and the development of empire.[14] Male writers who, as Janet Todd puts it, 'in their hypochondria, melancholia, sleeplessness or laziness, were in some way at odds with the energy if not the values of their society' may respond with increasing introversion and, hence, turn solipsistic and self-referential or choose to celebrate the alternative values of the melancholic in their work.[15] So, we have Thomas Warton's paean to *The Pleasures of Melancholy* in his poem of 1747; Gray's 'youth to Fortune and to Fame unknown' who was 'marked' by Melancholy 'for her own' (122–4); Collins, Chatterton and Cowper who made a poetics of isolation and self-reflection; and Werther, the wildly popular eponymous hero of Goethe's novel, who made suicide the appropriate aesthetic, if not logical, response of a sensitive man in a cruel world. It was partly Charlotte Smith's imitations of Werther in the *Sonnets*, along with numerous others by British poets, which helped to secure Werther's iconic status as melancholic man *par excellence*.

Whilst melancholy was largely associated with men, the equivalent pathology for women was hysteria. James's *Medical Dictionary* of 1743 characterizes hysteria as a shape shifter, a mutable opportunist that 'assumes the Appearance of almost every Distemper with which miserable Mortals are afflicted.'[16] While melancholy was understood as a response to the pressures of the social world, hysteria was unequivocally a disorder of sexual origin, the (apparently temporary) cure for which was marriage. According to James 'the Authorities of the greatest Physicians, concur in pronouncing Matrimony highly beneficial in removing hysteric Disorders'.[17] The expedience for the medical practitioner who could attribute all complaints of the female body to one irrefutable – because unexaminable – source (sexual disorder) and prescribe one socially convenient cure (marriage) can only be matched by the impact on women of having to understand all signs of physical illness as a symptom of acute internal irregularity, for which the cure would often be worse than the disease. While, as I have said, many male writers embraced the melancholic posture, turning their backs on a cruel world, it is understandable that women did not feel drawn to adopt the persona of the hysteric as a sign of their social rebellion, for as I have suggested hysteria was believed to be a response to sexual, not social, disorder. Perhaps the reason that Smith joins a tradition established by melancholic men is that she is keen to distance herself from the view that women's unhappiness is located in the female body. Given Charlotte

Smith's evident social conscience and keen eye for social satire, however, it is still perhaps odd that the sonnets are so solipsistic, even if that solipsism is, as I have argued, performative rather than expressive. There is, after all, precedent for the political sonnet in Milton's poetry, which was later adopted by Wordsworth. If, as I am arguing, she is not simply writing about her own personal sorrows, but writing of the condition of modern authorship, why did she choose such an introverted and arguably male tradition when her politics might have suited her for a more extrovert mode? To explore this question, I want to think about the character of melancholy by using more recent approaches to the term: to understand melancholy – and Smith's sonnets – not simply as a subjective response to personal loss, but as a condition of being a subject (and author) in modern culture. That is, I want to argue that Smith's melancholy *Elegiac Sonnets* are not a retreat from the world but a response to a culture that makes aliens of its authors.

MODERN AUTHORSHIP

In some ways, *The English Malady* and many eighteenth-century representations of the melancholic anticipate the approach to melancholy pioneered by Sigmund Freud. In his essay 'Mourning and Melancholia' Freud provides an account of the experience of loss. Distinguishing between the mourner and the melancholic, Freud describes the different responses to loss of each subject. His account is predicated upon the Oedipal myth of child development, whereby boys learn to relinquish their early sexual attachment to their mothers and to identify with their fathers and girls give up desire for their fathers for identification with their mothers. Freud's description of mourning (the process of separation from the lost object), and melancholia (the failure of the process of mourning), uses sexualized terms, recalling the fundamental stages of identity formation:

> [in mourning] the loved object no longer exists and it proceeds to demand that all libido shall be withdrawn from its attachments to that object...when the *work* of mourning is completed the ego becomes free and uninhibited again. [my italics][18]

I shall comment upon the significance of Freud's – or at least the translator's – use of the verb 'work' to describe the process of mourning, shortly. Here, suffice it to say that in melancholia, the work of mourning is incomplete. The melancholic remains attached to a lost, loved object, albeit at an unconscious level. The melancholic is neither free nor uninhibited.

Judith Hawley has argued that Smith's *Elegiac Sonnets* are melancholic in the Freudian sense.[19] They are not traditional elegies, Hawley suggests, because they resist the transcendence and consolation offered by the elegy. As such, they are melancholic, not mournful: 'Smith writes strange elegies because, instead of being able to renounce what she has lost, or to say farewell to the dead, she feels that she is entitled to have what she has lost restored to her.'[20] From Hawley's point of view, what Smith has lost – her children's inheritance and her social status – is identifiable and (so Smith would like to think) recoverable. But I would argue that it is the enigmatic, diffuse nature of the objects of loss in the sonnets that call to mind Freud's description of melancholia, which emphasizes less the object than the experience of loss:

> melancholia...may be the reaction to the loss of a loved object. Where the exciting causes are different one can recognize that there is a loss of a more ideal kind. The object has not perhaps actually died, but has been lost as an object of love.[21]

Some of Smith's sonnets *are* responses to the death of a 'loved object'. The speaker of Sonnet 78, 'Snowdrops', for instance, describes her inability to rejoice at the arrival of the snowdrops, the harbingers of spring.[22] The concluding five – as opposed to six – lines explain:

> Ah! ye soft, transient children of the ground,
> More fair was she on whose untimely grave
> Flow my unceasing tears! Their varied round
> The Seasons go; while I through all repine:
> For fixt regret, and hopeless grief are mine.
>
> (Curran, Sonnet 78, ll.10–14)

The speaker is locked in grief for the loss of 'she' who was more fair than the snowdrops. Whilst her loss of interest in the world around her – her inability to appreciate the snowdrops – is characteristic of the mourner, the '*unceasing* tears', '*fixt* regret,' and '*hopeless* grief', suggest the affliction is melancholia. This is number 78 of 92 *Elegiac Sonnets*, and the work of mourning does not seem to have begun, let alone have been completed. Nearly every poem, or short sequence such as the Werter poems, brings a new perspective on loss, though not necessarily a clear indication of what has been lost. As is characteristic of the literature of sensibility, it is the feeling, not its origin that is significant. Understanding this melancholy is easy in biographical terms, as Kennedy, Hawley and Fletcher argue. As I have suggested, Smith *invites* autobiographical readings of her poems in the prefaces to the numerous editions of the *Elegiac Sonnets*. When she writes that '[s]ome melancholy moments have been beguiled by expressing in verse the sensations those moments brought' (Curran, 3), she suggests that writing is a kind of therapy, a point argued by Deborah Kennedy. Here she anticipates by some years Wordsworth's 'emotion recollected in tranquility' and articulates the process of writing poetry as the evocation of feeling after the stimulus has passed. Significantly, while Wordsworth *recollects* the emotion – apparently leaving it unchanged – Smith *beguiles* it. This metaphor of seduction implies that the act of composition is an act of taking control, of transformation. The composition of a sonnet is a kind of emotional discipline, giving order to formless sensation. But as I have suggested, the sonnets bring us these fourteen lines of desolation over and over again. Whilst the work of mourning calls for sublimation of feelings of loss, the work of Smith's sonnets is to rearticulate them and, over the course of ten editions in sixteen years, to build up a repertoire of voices, analogies, similies, antonyms and locations to do so. This is less therapy – or as Hawley argues in generic terms, less the consolation and transcendence provided by the elegy – than a refusal to mourn. Why?

'Post-Freudian' theorists have drawn attention to the ideological nature of Freud's theories, arguing that the 'work' of mourning is a process that lends itself to the reintegration to society of healthy, productive subjects, 'free and uninhibited' to work.[23] The melancholic is, by implication, unhealthy, idle, and unproductive. This vocabulary is starkly visible in the comments of David M. Main, editor of a late nineteenth-century anthology of sonnets, which reproduced two of Smith's, 'Written at the

Close of Spring' and 'Should the lone wanderer, fainting on his way'.[24] He writes:

> The unmitigable woe with which Mrs Smith's poems are filled, together with their factitious and second-hand phraseology, renders them unpalatable to a generation so much *healthier* than that in which they were produced.[25]

In this robust Victorian dismissal of late eighteenth-century *ennui*, Main suggests that Smith's sonnets belong to a sickly generation. He does not dismiss Smith's worth entirely. Quoting from Smith's admirers, Wordsworth and Dyce, on the valuable qualities of her sonnets, Main writes that he has chosen 'an example of a different order, if not in all respects the best, certainly the most masculine and interesting of her poems': 'To the shade of Burns'.[26] Perhaps this poem appeals because it is about the dignity of the Scottish bard, and because the speaker talks of independence and liberty in such positive terms. If we consider Smith's sonnets as the *refusal* of the work of mourning, a refusal to sublimate feelings of loss and substitute the lost object, we can see how she anticipates and rejects the nineteenth-century predilection for healthy, masculine poetry. If Smith writes on the one hand to 'beguile' melancholy moments and to gain economic as well as emotional control, she writes with the knowledge that writing to live constitutes a loss of autonomy. The work of remunerated poets is melancholic, keeps them tied to an object of desire (autonomy) that always eludes them. Written alongside the novels that earn her keep, the sonnets record the losses of that living.

We can now understand Smith's sorrows in broader cultural terms, terms in which she seems to have understood her predicament and her writing. She lives, in Michel Foucault's terms, in an age of enlightenment whose ideal subject is governed by reason, is self-reliant and self-disciplined. Enlightenment culture is haunted by the fear of reason becoming diseased, dependent and undisciplined, hence the vilification of the leisured, the itinerant poor and the mad in much late eighteenth-century social commentary. Smith's enforced self-reliance and self-discipline lead her to fantasize about and envy rather than vilify the subjectivity of the leisured (Sonnet 81), the rural poor (Smith's recumbent woodman and shepherds) and the mad (Sonnet 70). She sees the lunatic of Sonnet 70

> more with envy than with fear;
> ... wildly wandering here,
> He seems (uncursed with reason) not to know
> The depth or the duration of his woe.
>
> (Curran, Sonnet 70, ll.10–14)

In 'post-Freudian', linguistic terms, subjects like the lunatic reside outside of the symbolic order, founded as it is on the repression and prohibition of bodily drives and desires that is compensated for by the entry into language. Thus, he makes 'hoarse, half-uttr'd lamentation' and 'murmuring responses to the dashing surf' (ll.7–8). Smith's idle rustics are significantly silent. Like Thomas Gray's 'mute inglorious Miltons' they do not speak, let alone write. Ideal and static, they are not granted the compromising subjectivity of Wordsworth's lyricists nor figured as part of a symbolic order to which Smith – who is so literally entrapped by a law that does not recognize her existence – cannot be reconciled.

There are moments of consolation in the sonnets. In particular, poems to friends or on friendship punctuate the ruminations on isolation and abjection (Sonnets 10, 19, 20, 28, 29, 34, 37, 48, 56, 81). But there is no progressive movement towards transcendence. One poem brings recovery, the next relapse. A wayward elegist, then, Smith will not get over her losses. Writing for remuneration is less therapy for the genteel Smith's sorrows than another source of her grief. It is a condition not peculiar to Smith's unusually difficult life but endemic to modern authorship. As I shall suggest in a later chapter, while consolation is not available in the *Sonnets*, and is certainly not achieved through the composition of the novels to which I turn next, a glimpse of hope is offered in one of her final poems, *Beachy Head*. Ironically, this poem, in which there are signs that the work of mourning was underway, was published after Smith's death.

2

Gossip and Politics in *Desmond*

Smith returned to England in 1785 and after further negotiations with her husband's creditors was able to settle her family in rented accommodation in Sussex, though they were to move frequently throughout Smith's life. She carried on writing poetry, but also turned her hand to translation.[1] In 1787, Smith and her husband separated. It was from around this time that Smith began writing fiction. Between 1788 and 1791 Cadell published the first three of her novels, the 'courtship' narratives *Emmeline*, *Ethelinde* and *Celestina*. Although there are points of social satire and critique of the lot of unpropertied women in each of these narratives, it was Smith's fourth novel, *Desmond*, published in 1792, that was to launch her reputation as a political writer.[2] Smith had made a brief visit to Paris part way through the composition of the novel and *Desmond* participates in the revolutionary debate as directly and polemically as any of her contemporary politicians who were exercised by events in France. That Smith turned to George Robinson for the publication of *Desmond* many have been a sign that her usual publisher Cadell were wary of its politics, but there may have been financial motives for the shift, as Smith's letters document some forthright exchanges between author and publisher on the subject of advances. As it was, *Desmond* did not make Smith much money, but it certainly drew attention to her as a novelist.

Desmond is Smith's only epistolary novel. There are references to and echoes of predecessors in the epistolary tradition: Sterne's *A Sentimental Journey* and *Tristram Shandy*; Burney's *Evelina*; Richardson's *Clarissa* and *Sir Charles Grandison*; Rousseau's *Julie, ou La Nouvelle Héloïse*; Goethe's *The Sorrows of Young Werther* and Sheridan's *The Memoirs of Miss Sidney Bidulph*. In Smith's novel the primary correspondence is between the guileless protagonist

Lionel Desmond, and his erstwhile guardian and world-weary mentor Erasmus Bethel. Their letters chart what the wry Bethel sees as Desmond's 'wild and romantic passion' (*D*, 53) for Geraldine Verney, a married mother of three and model of wifely duty and selflessness, and the young idealist's 'romantic and...patriotic journey to France'(*D*, 53) at the start of the French Revolution. The reader is invited to share some of Bethel's satirical view of Desmond's amorous and political romances, as Desmond often writes bathetically of Geraldine and France as two lovers who demand his attention: 'there is not in the world another [subject than Geraldine] that really fixes my attention an instant: not one that has any momentary attraction, unless it be the transactions in France' (*D*, 67). Just as in her *Letters from France* Helen Maria Williams uses romantic vignettes to illustrate the political romance of the revolution, so, in Desmond's eyes, the plight of Geraldine in thrall to a licentious aristocrat is a microcosmic version of the sufferings of the French people under the *ancien régime*.

Smith may have put together her first epistolary novel just as the form was becoming outmoded, but there is another context of letters to which *Desmond* speaks. The early 1790s saw a flurry of publications relating to the events in France, many of which were published in the form of private letters. What is now known as the 'revolution debate' was sparked off by a lecture given by the dissenter Richard Price on the anniversary of the Glorious Revolution in 1688. The erstwhile Whig liberal Edmund Burke, who was alarmed at the course of events in France and at Price's comparison of the French with the English revolution, was moved to reply, and composed his *Reflections on the Revolution in France* (1790) to mount a defence of the British constitution, monarchy and aristocracy.[3] The replies to Burke came over the course of the next couple of years and included Mary Wollstonecraft's *A Vindication of the Rights of Men* (1790), and her later *A Vindication of the Rights of Woman* (1792), Thomas Paine's *Rights of Man* (1791) and James Mackintosh's *Vindicae Gallicae* (1791). There were fictional responses too. *Desmond* is both a reply to Burke's *Reflections* and a dramatization and 'privatization' of the revolution debate, drawing it into the domestic and romantic affairs of its protagonists. Bethel and Desmond stand as the Burkean elder statesman and the idealistic correspondent of the *Reflections*. Political debate is conveyed not just in Desmond's polemical exchanges with Bethel, however, but in the gossip and ill-informed prejudice of the minor characters like the Fairfaxes, the Misses Elford, Danby and General Wallingford.

GOSSIP AND POLITICAL MISREPRESENTATION

'Gossip' is dominantly associated with private exchanges and, as Blakey Vermeule has suggested 'relentlessly favors [sic] some kinds of information over other kinds. Sexual scandal, cheating, sudden windfalls, dramatic successes, spectacular failures, and social climbing'.[4] In this light, people do not strictly 'gossip' about politics, but, as Smith's novel illustrates, the language of politics is riven with gossip. Just as the romance plot in *Desmond* is coterminous with the political commentary, sharing as they do themes of seduction, betrayal and the intransigence of social prejudice, so the register of gossip and casual speculation is offered as a mirror and extension of formal political debate. Burke's *Reflections* has a register of avuncular familiarity but is laced with salacious speculations on the characters of the revolutionaries and their British acolytes. Thus Richard Price, caricatured by Burke as an 'archpontiff of the rights of men',[5] is in the sensationalist logic of *Reflections* complicit with the revolutionary party's 'authorizing [of] treasons, robberies, rapes, assassinations, slaughters, and burnings' throughout France.[6] The defamatory tone of Burke's text is picked up and used by his adversaries, most notably Mary Wollstonecraft in her intemperate political epistle, *A Vindication of the Rights of Men* in which she attacks the person as much as the politics of the great British statesman for his vanity, ambition and 'teeming fancy'.[7]

Desmond, written in 1792 and set between June 1790 and February 1792, emerges from this context of political slanging match and the grave historical events that sparked it off. These were the years when the French National Assembly made its democratic mark by, amongst other measures, eradicating the titles of hereditary nobility, taking church property into the ownership of the state, abolishing sovereign courts and replacing them with elected judges and tribunals and removing censorship from French newspapers. The new freedoms of this rapidly expanding French press meant that word about such decrees spread rapidly, and made its way over the Channel within days of their inception. Smith's novel captures the gossipy reception of news about the revolution in England, and has its liberal protagonists – Desmond, Montfleuri, Geraldine and to some degree Bethel – rail against the apparent misrepresentations of French reform in the British press. For instance, in a letter from Paris, dated 19 July 1790, Desmond writes to Bethel of 'the animating spectacle of the 14th', the Fête de la Fédération. Sounding very much like Smith's contemporary, Helen Maria Williams in her *Letters From France*, Desmond assures Bethel that:

> Nothing is more unlike the real state of this country, than the accounts which have been given of it in England; and that the sanguinary and ferocious democracy, the scenes of anarchy and confusion, which we have had so pathetically described and lamented, have no existence but in the malignant fabrications of those who have been paid for their mis-representations... (*D*, 87)

According to Desmond, these misrepresentations are peddled not just by the press but by men in the pay of the government who 'believe the delusion of the people necessary to their own views' (*D*, 87). Like Williams' persona in her *Letters*, Desmond offers himself as the conduit of transparent truths about France and the revolution, a beacon in the darkness of misrepresentation and political gossip. The gossips who, from Desmond's point of view, misrepresent the course of events in France, have gullible audiences 'unable or unwilling to distinguish declamation from argument, or prejudice from reason' (*D*, 81). Gossip of course abounds in its natural domestic habitat and here it is women who exceed in the discourse. Miss Elford, in Fanny Waverly's terms, a 'shrivelled, satirical Sybil' (*D*, 217) is the most accomplished gossip. Fanny, taking up the tools of her oppressor in a vitriolic letter to her sister, reports how Miss Elford and a young physician are to be married: 'I really wish they may, if it be only in the hope, that Miss Elford, in having a husband of her own, will be so engaged by her own unexpected good fortune, as to let the rest of the world remain for some time unmolested' (*D*, 217).

The distortion of historical events in the novel occurs in print and in the daily round of social encounters. Readings of political events are filtered through the lens of social prejudice and taste for sensation. When Desmond visits Bethel's relatives the Fairfaxes, where the gouty General Wallingford, who resembles 'a garden set on its end, and supported by two legs' (*D*, 70) reports on the decree passed by the National Assembly abolishing titles (*D*, 73–4), the ensuing exchange between the General, Lord Newminster and Mrs Fairfax gives voice to the 'unofficial' counter-revolutionary opinion of the British gentry. Mrs Fairfax's indignant defence of hereditary titles articulates a populist fear of the mob that has its 'official' political origin in the 'swinish multitude' of Burke's *Reflections*:

> A title is as much a person's property as his estate; and, in my mind, one might as well be taken away as another – And to lose one's very birth-right, by a mob too, of vulgar creatures. – Good heaven! I declare the very idea is excessively terrific: only suppose the English mob were to get such a notion, and in some odious riot, begin the same sort of thing here! (*D*, 73)

The loyalist Wallingford had earlier hinted at this fear of the mob when he lamented the destruction of Paris as a pleasurable haunt for the 'man of fashion' (*D*, 70), remarking that from his leisured perspective as a 'grand tourist', 'the people had liberty enough' (*D*, 70). The views of Newminster, who for most of the scene is prostrate on a sofa, fawning over a pair of dogs, are the least measured and most anti-democratic: ' "Rot the people," – cried the noble Peer. "I wish they were all hanged out of the way, both in France and here too" ' (*D*, 71). The crudeness of Newminster's outburst prompts a more sentimental reflection from Mrs Fairfax on the consequences of revolutionary 'levelling' and the plight of the fallen French nobility:

> how my sympathising heart bleeds, when I reflect on the numbers of amiable people of rank, compelled thus to the cruel necessity of resigning those ancient and honourable names which distinguished them from the vulgar herd! (*D*, 71)

Commentators on Smith's 1792 poem *The Emigrants*, written as Smith's response to the sight of exiled French aristocrats arriving on English shores, attribute to the author a Fairfaxian sympathy with nobility, and read the poem as a corrective to the radicalism of *Desmond*. As I argue in my reading of that poem, however, Smith does not apologetically take up an 'anti-mob' position but offers a revisionary reading of nobility. Nobility is not to be found in 'Pensioners/Of base corruption, who, in quick ascent/To opulence unmerited, become giddy with pride' (*TE*, I, ll.316–18), the 'bought' British peers like Newminster but in the French *émigrés*. The 'vulgar mob' of whom Wallingford, Fairfax and Newminster speak are for Smith, even by 1792, a 'raging multitude, to madness stung' (*TE*, I, l.334) because 'oppress'd too long' (*TE*, I, l.333). Smith's redefiniton of 'the mob' and nobility against the tide of counter-revolutionary reaction, runs throughout her texts (we see it in *The Old Manor House* with Orlando's negotiation with 'chivalry') and is evidenced mostly in this novel in Desmond's discourse.

Desmond is mostly silent in the scene referred to above, and reserves his opinion on the French abolition of titles for a conversation with Miss Fairfax. The younger woman shares her mother's sense of shock at the apparent collapse of social hierarchy in France and her dismay 'that nobility and fashion are quite destroyed' (*D*, 72). When Desmond counters her view of the 'frightful news', feeling himself 'much more disposed to rejoice at, than to lament it' (*D*, 73), he finds himself ostracized from the Fairfaxes' polite company. The radical Desmond is deemed by this circle at least to be irredeemably vulgar, no better than 'a common country 'Squire' (*D*, 74). Desmond's riposte and lament that the 'common country 'Squire[s]' are a 'race of men...almost, if not entirely annihilated in England... [effected by] a total change of manners' (*D*, 74) marks out his Painite credentials as a defender of democracy and meritocracy. '[I]f all those who are now raised above us by their names' he hypothesizes to Miss Fairfax 'were to have no other distinction than their merits would the...truly noble among them...be less beloved and revered if they were known only by their family names?' (*D*, 74).[8]

REWRITING THE SEDUCTION NARRATIVE

The novel vindicates Desmond's attack on hereditary privilege in its portrait of the rakish Verney, his British companions and their

French equivalents de Boisbelle and de Romagnecourt. Verney, described by Geraldine's sister Fanny as a 'man of fortune and family' who has thrown away both, threatens to make Geraldine 'liable to all the distresses and inconveniences of poverty' (D, 229) by selling her to the highest bidder. The threat of sexual and social fall that pursues but is ultimately averted by Geraldine is a standard aspect of the seduction narratives of eighteenth-century domestic novels. The novel anticipates Geraldine's fate in its early depiction of Louisa, wife of the young Bethel. Louisa, the Welsh, country-bred niece of Bethel's solicitor, Stamford, captivates Bethel with 'her total unconsciousness of the beauty she so eminently possessed' (D, 63) and he marries her. Once introduced to London life, however, Louisa lives 'in a constant succession of flattery' (D, 64) and succumbs to the seduction of 'a man who disgraces the name he bears' (D, 65), eventually following him to France. Bethel tells the story of Louisa to warn Desmond of the dangers of romantic passion, but the narrative has broader targets. The characterization of Robert Stamford provides a stronger example than the foppish Newminster of the wrongs of bought entitlement. Stamford flatters Bethel into taking up one of two seats in Parliament, for a borough that belonged to the latter, and Stamford becomes the beneficiary of the other. Eager for recognition, Stamford, 'the country attorney, was soon forgotten, in Stamford the confident of ministers, and the companion of peers' (D, 64), whilst Bethel comes increasingly under his control. Stamford's moral descent is exemplified when Bethel reveals that is was he who sold the 'person of his niece to her seducer with as much *sang froid* as he had before sold his own conscience to the minister' (D, 65). Louisa is not the only one seduced by flattery. Bethel's is a two-pronged fable of political and amorous seduction, and he offers Desmond the wisdom of his experience. In his political career, he professes to have seen 'such decided selfishness in all parties, so little sincerity, so little real concern for the general good in any, that it imprest me with an universal mistrust of all who profess the science of politics' (D, 123). Disillusioned in love, Bethel is moved to recommend to Desmond women like the Fairfaxes on the anti-pastoral grounds that they 'are much less likely to sacrifice their honour on the altar of vanity, than the rural damsel from the Welch mountains or northern fells' (D, 66).

The novel's marriage of private and public in the *rapprochement* of romance and political narrative is echoed at a formal level in the merging of 'official' and 'unofficial' discourses on public life, as discussed above. The epistolary mode of course lends itself to the circulation of gossip, half-truth and speculations. Although most events are focalized through Desmond, there is no omniscient narrator who divulges the full story to us as we proceed, so the reader must weave the incidents and episodes narrated in each letter into a coherent whole. Thus, we have the version of France peddled in booksellers and drawing rooms, and 'eye-witness' accounts from Desmond and Geraldine. Omniscient narrator or none, only a reader as weak-minded as Geraldine's vacillating brother Waverley could fail to see whose political views carry most weight. The reader is left in more doubt, however, about the full facts of the 'love plot', as Desmond's role as vehicle of transparent truths becomes obscured as the novel proceeds. The end of Volume 2 sees Geraldine temporarily ensconced in lodgings in Herefordshire, where, for a while unknown to her, she is under the benevolent watch of Desmond and, later, the more malevolent eye of Verney's associate de Romagnecourt, to whom Geraldine has effectively been sold. Although the threat of her abduction to France is averted, Geraldine soon finds herself on the way across the Channel to meet her errant husband. While we read letters from Geraldine in France, her whereabouts are thrown into doubt by reports that Geraldine has been seen again in Herefordshire. In a letter to Bethel, Fanny recounts her mother's outburst that Geraldine:

> is not in France, perhaps never has been there; but has been, and is, I believe, in my conscience, still at the farm-house in Herefordshire, where she lived before – where she has lain-in – yes, Miss, lain-in of a girl, and is the declared mistress of that villain, Desmond, who has been there with her; and, perhaps, is with her yet. (*D*, 352)

The volume of qualifiers in this account reveal the speaker's uncertainty, but Fanny is less hesitant in attributing the source of the material to Miss Elford, who, disappointed in love, is back to molesting 'the rest of the world' (*D*, 217).

MISTAKEN IDENTITY

Desmond is at this point deliberately concealing *his* whereabouts from Bethel and Geraldine, and although discerning readers, like Bethel and Fanny, do not believe the gossips, the truth of the situation is not yet clear. There have been hints, however. Desmond's relationship with Josephine de Boisbelle, the sister of Desmond's French pro-revolutionary friend Montfleuri, is represented by Bethel as the perfect distraction for his lovelorn friend. Desmond himself represents Josephine as, not unlike Geraldine, 'very beautiful and very unhappy, two circumstances that cannot fail to make her extremely interesting' (*D*, 110). Despite Desmond's protestations of his undying attachment to Geraldine, and the fact that Josephine is also married, we eventually learn, in the novel's penultimate letter from Montfleuri to Bethel, how Josephine's brother 'encourage[d], in the gay and unguarded heart of my sister de Boisbelle, an affection for Desmond' (*D*, 410), and that this affection produced a baby. Montfleuri is at pains to exempt Desmond from blame for 'it was her unguarded folly, and not to any art or deception on his part, that the blame was owing' (*D*, 411). It is Josephine, attended by Montfleuri, not Geraldine and Desmond, who are spotted at the Herefordshire cottage.

This case of mistaken identity obviously draws attention to the similarity of Geraldine and Josephine. Both are, in Desmond's terms, virtuous women, married to libertines.[9] Josephine functions as a Gothic double for Geraldine, not as an evil *alter ego*, but as a woman who gives way to 'unguarded' feeling whilst the other adheres to the point of self-annihilation to her sense of 'duty'. In the persons of these two women, Smith rewrites the seduction plot twice: Geraldine escapes from the clutches of numerous would-be seducers, her husband dies and she is allowed to reconcile duty with desire in her union with Desmond. Josephine, the 'fallen' woman, is given the chance of a new life.

In terms of the gender politics of the novel, Geraldine's acceptance of Desmond's child and Josephine's sanguine resignation of his affection may seem conservative, a resigned acceptance of 'duty'. When read in the context of more conventional 'seduction narratives' however, like Frances

Sheridan's 1761 novel *Memoirs of Miss Sidney Bidulph*, Geraldine and Desmond's eventual union looks positively unbridled. Sidney Bidulph is betrothed to the man of her desires, Faulkland, only to discover an earlier 'attachment' (Miss Burchill) and the child of that union. Although all the evidence points to his blamelessness and the seductive powers of his mistress and her aunt, Sidney is convinced that his duty is to Miss Burchill. Although Faulkland is finally freed from Miss Burchill, he subsequently kills himself and Sidney is left only with the knowledge that she did her duty. Smith's novel, on the contrary, kills off one errant husband, Verney, and probably a second, de Boisbelle,[10] and unearths a first love for Josephine, 'a naval officer, a near relation' (*D*, 410) stationed in the East Indies, thereby freeing up Geraldine and Desmond. Geraldine is not only liberated by her husband's death but by his final wishes. In a deathbed reformation scene, Verney gives his blessing and legal sanction to Desmond's union with his wife, and dictates a memorandum 'expressing his wishes, that if ever [Geraldine] took a second husband, it might be his friend Desmond' (*D*, 408).

With Geraldine free to express her desires with the sanction of her husband, Desmond's past indiscretion needs to be exonerated. Smith manages this by the logic of transparency, the much-celebrated virtue of liberal sensibility. In his letter to Bethel, Montfleuri writes that Josephine 'told me he had promised nothing; that he used no art to betray her; but, on the contrary, had told her that his whole soul was dedicated to another' (*D*, 411). However, in an environment where social conduct is under minute surveillance and where actions, let alone motives, are open to endless reinterpretations, Montfleuri considers it 'rational to conceal what could not be amended' (*D*, 411) and removes Josephine to the house in Herefordshire, where she is, perhaps conveniently, mistaken for Geraldine.

With Josephine's consenting to Geraldine having her child and Verney's consenting to Desmond having Geraldine, a new 'democratically sanctioned' family is put together. In an obvious nod to the new political order in France, liberalism is in the ascendant over libertinism. In his final euphoric letter to Bethel, Desmond imagines his future with 'My Geraldine – You, my dear Bethel – your sweet Louisa – my friend Montfleuri, and his

Fanny. – I imagine the delight of living in that tender confidence of mutual affection, which only such a circle of friends can taste' (*D*, 414). There is no place in this enlightened circle, however, for Josephine, who has been dispatched to Italy and must wait uncertainly for confirmation of her husband's death and the possible return from the East Indies of her first love. Even then, Montfleuri is guarded in his expectations for her future: 'it is probable that their first attachment will end in a marriage; but I shall never deceive him as to what has happened in his absence' (*D*, 411). Montfleuri's new-found commitment to transparency may do Josephine few favours.

There are no letters from Josephine, which reinforces her status as a cipher, a temporary receptacle for Desmond's desires until Geraldine becomes available. That she is not condemned is testament to the radicalism of Smith's novel, its resistance to the logic of the gossips; that she is left out of the new order suggests Smith's own doubts about the radicalism, for women, of that new order which has its own modes of surveillance and sanction. As we will see, in Helen Maria Williams' *Julia*, there are similar misgivings about the implications for women of a culture of transparency; misgivings that, I shall argue, see Williams retreat to a more conservative model of female conduct than has been claimed for the novel.

3

Declarations of Independence in *The Old Manor House*

Charlotte Smith's fifth novel, *The Old Manor House* was published in 1793, and won Smith back some friends after the critical and political fallout from *Desmond*.[1] While the *Analytical Review* and the *Critical Review* criticized the novel's improbabilities of plot, its cluttered and circuitous narrative and its lack of moral decorum, the novel gradually accumulated readers and critical support.[2]

Contemporary critics have defended the novel's apparent formal inconsistencies by drawing attention to Smith's playfulness with the romance genre and her ability to match form to content. Jacqueline Labbe, for instance, argues that the shift in narrative pace after the first volume, which perplexed and alienated some early reviewers, can be accounted for by the accelerated pace of events in the life of the protagonist, Orlando Somerive. The 'leisured' first volume, she writes, 'explores the relaxed setting of Orlando's youth' while the style of the subsequent volumes reflects the more complicated and rushed nature of his life (*TOMH*, 13). Joseph Bartolomeo has drawn attention to Smith's 'parodic self-consciousness about the conventions of romance as they operate in the novel', defending *The Old Manor House* both from early critics who questioned the probability of some narrative developments and from some late twentieth-century feminist critics who regarded the novel as conservative in sexual politics, conforming to 'the standards of the sentimental love story or the extravagant romance'.[3] Labbe and Bartolomeo agree that Smith's representation of Orlando Somerive is often critical and throws into question the status of the novel's central love plot and the novel's relationship to the genre of romance. This critical distance from Orlando, Labbe and Bartolomeo suggest, creates an ironic frame for the novel's denouement in which the woman and the property from which the 'hero' is separated for much of the novel are restored, or rather, granted to him. We are asked to question rather than revel in Orlando's successes. I would agree with Labbe and Bartolomeo that Orlando Somerive is an ambiguous romance hero. However, I see his failed heroism less as a critical response to the genre of romance than as a continuation of Smith's critique of the British public sphere and British masculinity.

MORE REFLECTIONS

The Old Manor House is set in the 1770s, the decade of the American Revolution and the Declaration of Independence that severed the allegiance of the thirteen colonized states of America to the British Crown. Part of the action takes place on the American east coast, as the protagonist Orlando Somerive joins a failing British military effort to subdue the rebels. Most contemporaneous critics regarded this retreat into the recent past as Smith's chastened response to the criticism she faced for the openly topical politics of her previous novel *Desmond*. That novel had fictionalized the responses of the British public to the revolution debate, and ultimately vindicated the radical position. It did so by dramatizing what was at stake in the private domain as it charted the abuse suffered by Geraldine Verney at the hands of her libertine husband and offered a sympathetic view of her relationship with the liberal intellectual, pro-revolutionary Lionel Desmond. If Smith was now intent on taking a more conservative line by offering a more conventional romance and avoiding topical debate, why did she serve up another response to the immediate present in her long poem *The Emigrants*, published in the same year as *The Old Manor House* and which offered a damning critique of the British establishment? Far from retreating to a quieter politics, *The Old Manor House* provides a trenchant critique of the British military action in America and represents British society in a state of decay and corruption. Rather than displace the politics of the present, Smith draws attention to some alarming continuities between Britain in the 1770s and the 1790s: an attachment to feudal property arrangements, cultural medievalism and chivalric notions of gender relations, all of which, of course, had been served up as the stuff with which to defend Britain in Edmund Burke's *Reflections*.[4] Smith had demonstrated her familiarity with Burke's arguments in *Desmond*, and *The Old Manor House* presents us with another take on the *Reflections*. The novel presents us with a portrait of the Britain that Burke was so keen to defend but deconstructs his image of political stability and benign social hierarchy. To understand the relationship between property and politics in *The Old Manor House*, it is instructive to look at a passage from *Reflections*, which sets out Burke's defence of hereditary property and political representation:

> Nothing is a due and adequate representation of a state, that does not represent its ability, as well as its property. But as ability is a vigorous and active principle, and as property is sluggish, inert, and timid, it can never be safe from the invasions of ability, unless it be, out of all proportion, predominant in the representation.[5]

The Old Manor House, as recent critics have pointed put, critiques the system of hereditary property ownership.[6] It does so by mobilizing Burke's terms ironically, pitting the 'sluggishness' of property and its political representatives against the active principle of ability. 'Property' is represented by those who have it (Grace Rayland, Belgrave, Stockton and Tracy) and those who live in hope of inheriting it (principally, the Somerives). 'Ability' is represented by the politically disenfranchised: the servants of Rayland Hall, especially the women Betsy Richards and Monimia Morysine, and by their thematic equivalent, Britain's unrepresented subjects in America.

ROMANCE AND HISTORY

Smith's contemporary critics focused less on the politics of the novel than on its romance plot – or they failed to make the connection between the two – and in this respect they followed the lead of Smith's central characters who pay little attention to contemporary politics. Grace Rayland, the antediluvian owner of Rayland Hall and a parody of the medievalism of the late eighteenth century, 'talked much of modern immorality and dissipation' but:

> knew very little of modern manners, seldom seeing any of those people who are what is called people of the world; and forming her ideas of what was passing in it, only from newspapers and the Lady's Magazine, or some such publication, which excited only wonder and disgust – (*TOMH*, 265)

Orlando and the rest of the Somerives are too preoccupied with the attempt to win over Grace Rayland to take an interest in events much beyond Rayland Hall. The 'modern' men of property and political influence – the boorish and corrupt Stockton and Belgrave – show little more concern or insight. At a dinner hosted by Stockton for Orlando and his father 'the last news from America was discussed; but as they all agreed in one sentiment – that the rebellious colonists ought to be extirpated – there was no room for argument, and the discourse soon languished; and then revived on topics nearer home' (*TOMH*, 170). Of the novel's propertied representatives of 'public life' it is only the ageing dandy General Tracy who understands the implications of the American situation.

The fashionable General Tracy accrues authority over Orlando's family. He is able to persuade Orlando to take up a commission (in order to ingratiate himself with the family and to clear his way to the eldest Somerive daughter, Isabella) because of his ability to read and conceal historical reality. Tracy knows that the war between Britain and America is escalating, but convinces the Somerives 'that those wretched, ragged fellows, without discipline, money, clothes, or arms, will be unable longer to struggle for their chimerical liberty' and are probably 'by this time crushed' (*TOMH*, 160). Tracy's power over the Somerives is dependent upon their enervation, a sluggishness bred from their dependence on their propertied relation, Grace Rayland. They all give up responsibility for their futures and fall prey to the machinations of Tracy.

CONSUMERIST POWER

A contrast to their passivity comes in the figure of a marginal character, the under servant Betty or Betsy Richards. Like Tracy,

Betty is a competent reader of the modern world, if not the political world then at least the world of fashion, and this gives her a surprising degree of private, if not public, power. Like Grace Rayland, she reads the *Lady's Magazine*, but unlike her mistress she embraces its guidance on modern sartorial trends in an attempt to break out of her life below stairs. Smith's witty characterization of Betty draws her out from the marginal world of servants into the centre of the narrative in the first volume and as a foil for the demure heroine, Monimia. Monimia, the niece, or possibly the illegitimate daughter of the forbidding housekeeper of the Hall, Mrs Lennard, has as little status in the household as Betty (in Monimia's words, 'Betty is, like myself, a very friendless orphan, a poor girl that my aunt has taken from the parish' (*TOMH*, 74)), but the novel allows them both to escape servitude by virtue of different forms of feminine 'ability': Betty's consumerist power of sartorial self-transformation and the sentimental Monimia's exceptional inner self, 'her native rectitude of heart and generosity of spirit' (*TOMH*, 75). There is much emphasis on the difference in dress between the two girls. In the tradition of the eighteenth-century Magdelen girls, Monimia is dressed to display Mrs Rayland's charity: 'not in gauzes or flounces...but in a plain stuff...a plain cap, and a clean white apron, that she might never be encouraged to vanity by any kind of finery that did not become her situation' (*TOMH*, 47). Betty, the 'country coquette' (*TOMH*, 82) revels in the 'the ribbands,...the flowered shawls, the bugle necklaces, and caps with new edging to them' (*TOMH*, 82) bestowed on her by the enamoured butler Patterson. Betty's taste for fashion is associated with the broader thematics of autonomy and independence. She tellingly dresses her hair according to the styles represented in a 'certain pocket-book...which represented in one of its leaves "six young ladies in the most fashionable head-dresses for 1776"' (*TOMH*, 83). Sartorial extravagance is Betty's declaration of independence.

While Monimia is overawed by Betty (she 'knew not how to refuse her any thing' (*TOMH*, 83)) and Orlando is alarmed by her flightiness, Betty is not vilified in Smith's narrative. Her ability to acquire the power to consume and accrue fashionable goods might easily have been used by Smith to exemplify her suspect morality or at least her vulnerability to sexual exploitation, thus throwing into relief Monimia's chastity and integrity. Indeed, Betty seems set for the standard fate of the seduced country girl of sentimental narrative as, like a young Moll Flanders, she falls for the temptations of the city: 'There's Mr Pattenson always a-telling me, that handsome girls have no occasion to be drudges as I be, or as I have been; for that in London they make their fortunes, and live like the finest ladies of the land' (*TOMH*, 110). Betty does go to London to make her fortune, but avoids the traditional fate of 'the fallen woman'. She escapes from Rayland Hall as Philip's mistress, but when he is removed to Fleet Prison for unpaid debts, Betty moves on. A chance encounter outside a haberdasher's shop between Orlando and Betty finds her fresh from a visit to her erstwhile seducer but now 'under the protection of another person' (*TOMH*, 442). The scene re-establishes the connection between Betty's taste for fashion and her quasi-independence (it is her new lover who provides her with the means to 'make some purchases before she went to her lodgings in Charlotte Street' (*TOMH*, 442)). Smith's reluctance to accede to a more repressive sexual morality and to punish Betty's refusal to 'be always a slave' and to dare 'to stir ever so little' (*TOMH*, 110) adds nuance to the treatment of 'consumer culture' in Smith's novel. While she condemns the descent to consumerism in the public sphere, as represented by the self-interested Belgrave, Stockton and Tracy, and their ability to augment their hereditary power with the purchase of privilege and further political influence, she acknowledges that the power to consume is one of the only means of exerting influence available to the lower-class woman, or indeed any woman who has a tenuous hold on the true means of political power, property.

Superficially, Betty is Monimia's 'other', but in drawing attention to their interchangeability (Betty and Monimia are repeatedly mistaken for one another, or at least suspicion falls on Betty as the woman involved in trysts with Orlando), Smith is able to expose Orlando's suspect morality (reinforced at other points in the novel where he is mistaken for his dissolute elder brother). Monimia resists the comparison between herself and Betty and reflects with regret on the clandestine meetings with Orlando that have put her 'in the way of being believed no better than the servant... How could I bear to be thought of by others as I think of her!' (*TOMH*, 221). Betty sees their interchangeability in lighter terms. When Orlando gives her a shilling for waiting up to give him access to the study where he will meet Monimia, she supposes 'they as bides with you in your study have double price' (*TOMH*, 151). Betty assumes that Monimia is paid for her services just as she is, first by Pattensen, then by Philip, and later by 'Mr Filmer'. Betty's insouciant observation about Monimia's possible financial recompense highlights Orlando's inability to provide for Monimia at all. While Betty's sexual liaisons offer her a limited kind of freedom (as a consumer and sexual agent) Monimia's relationship with Orlando, initially at least, pushes her further into servitude and dependency: 'She was on his account a prisoner, for he learned that when he was not in the country she was allowed more liberty' (*TOMH*, 59). As we will see, it is Monimia's 'ability' rather than Orlando's sluggish chivalry that eventually liberates her.

INSURRECTION

Betty's assertion of her independence is just one example of the insurrection 'below stairs' in Rayland Hall, for in a 'great house there are among the servants as many cabals, and as many schemes, as among the leaders of a great nation' (*TOMH*, 83). The housekeeper Mrs Lennard, the daughter of a merchant whose business collapsed during the South Sea Bubble of 1720, is welcomed into the Hall as the companion of Mrs Rayland, 'whose pride was gratified in having about her the victim of unsuccessful trade, for which she had always a most profound contempt' (*TOMH*, 43). However, Mrs Rayland may be the patron, but Lennard has the real authority in the house and has designs on a large share of the Rayland estate. Pattenson, the libertine butler, has somehow accumulated great wealth while in Mrs Rayland's service and expects to acquire more on her death. A third favourite, the coachman Snelcraft, enjoys the fruits of his trade in contraband goods (using the cellars in the Hall for storage) and plans to marry off his daughter to Orlando if he comes into the estate. Mrs Rayland's inattention to the activities of her servants is linked thematically to the broader ignorance in the novel about the British subjects across the Atlantic; 'a subject with which, at that time, men not in parliament and their families supposed they had nothing to do' (*TOMH*, 262). Mrs Rayland's belief in her own status as absolute feudal overseer depends on this separation of the public and the private. She sees her power in the household as private and certainly unconnected with the mores of a modern world that she despises. However, in the 1790s it is not possible to understand the 'old manor house' as a purely private hierarchy. The meaning of the 'old house' is over-determined by Burke's metaphor of the 'old establishment' or house of the British constitution that has survived because of conservative restoration not rapid modernization.[7] For Burke, the house of England has benefited from a 'slow...imperceptible' makeover, a reformation guided by 'circumspection and caution'.[8] Smith parodies Burke's symbolism. Rayland Hall is collapsing from its foundations because of its backward-looking proprietor. After her death and the exile of the heir, Orlando, the physical fabric of the house rapidly disintegrates. Orlando returns to a gothic ruin: doors off their hinges, falling wainscots and rotting floorboards (*TOMH*, 400–1). What Burke warns may happen at the hand of revolutionaries has already happened at the hands of England's backward-looking families of property and an acquisitive new middle class (the self-serving Hollybourns, representatives of the clergy and their unscrupulous stewards the Rokers, symbols of the much-reviled legal system). Arguably, the restoration of the Hall to Orlando Somerive arrests the decay and sets in train the Burkean ideal of gradual renovation. Orlando restores the old manor house 'without spoiling that look of venerable antiquity for which it was so remarkable' (*TOMH*, 521).

BURKEAN MAN

Orlando is indeed in many ways the model Burkean man: he bears the 'sullen resistance to innovation' (he is perplexed by modernity) and 'the cold sluggishness of our national character...the stamp of our forefathers'.[9] He is chivalrous, cautious and circumspect. But as I have suggested, Smith's novel does not underwrite the Burkean analogy. She uses his imagery to deconstruct his myth of Englishness. Orlando proves, in fact, to be a caricature of the Burkean ideal. In Orlando, chivalry, caution and circumspection are rewritten as quixotism, prevarication and idleness.

Orlando is named after Ariosto's love-struck hero and under the tutelage of Mrs Rayland he learns to live according to the laws of romance. He constructs Monimia as a romance heroine: innocent, inaccessible and dependent on his services for her education and her liberty. Even in their early encounters, however, Smith draws attention to the partiality of his reading of Monimia. While he constructs her as the passive recipient of his favours (Thisbe to his Pyramus, Galatea to his Pygmalion, Miranda to Ferdinand) she repeatedly demonstrates her ability to act independently of Orlando's assistance. When he penetrates her turret, it is Monimia who cuts through the hangings to ease his access (*TOMH*, 64). When they are nearly discovered by Philip, Orlando casts 'towards Monimia a look of anguish and terror' while Monimia retains 'her presence of mind' and concocts a plan of action (*TOMH*, 224).

Monimia's presence of mind, her constancy and ability to act under pressure are all the more necessary because of Orlando's vacillations and his malleability. As a second son, Orlando is treated as a cipher by his family: he is 'not Philip', and is handed over to Mrs Rayland in exchange for the family fortune. Mrs Rayland treats him as her knight-errant, an identity he readily internalizes and acts out. He accedes to General Tracy's designs, takes a commission and becomes a pawn in a conflict played out, Smith suggests, for profit and not, as Orlando romantically wants to believe, for the moral right of his country (*TOMH*, 353). The apotheosis of Orlando's romantic self-determination and self-belief is his sojourn in America where he is repeatedly taken prisoner and undergoes a series of physical transformations. In an inversion of Betty's sartorial empowerment, Orlando is gradually divested of the self that resides in his external appearance. When he is captured by the Iroquois his military garb is swapped for the dress of 'an Indian warrior...and he was distinguished from an Iroquois by nothing but his English complexion' (*TOMH*, 382). Under the watch of Wolfhunter, Orlando is guided to Quebec, where he is temporarily 'once more restored to the appearance of an Englishman' (*TOMH*, 391) and sets off for home via New York. Again his journey is intercepted and he is taken off his course, this time by French naval officers. Disembarking in France, he finds his passage home is blocked by the lack of 'open communication between France and England' (*TOMH*, 393). His only option is to travel with French smugglers. The hero returns as contraband goods.

Orlando's inability to determine the direction and speed of his passage is symptomatic of the lack of agency of the British soldiers caught up in the conflict but is also consistent with Orlando's ever-diminishing will and control over his own destiny. His loss of identity on his circuitous journey home is externalized by the gradual removal of his clothes and personal belongings by those who take him captive. The fishermen take 'a very good hat' in exchange for an 'old one' which 'seemed only half a hat' and the buckles from his shoes; he lost his 'great coat' to the Iroquois; his waistcoat is 'the only part of his dress that was the same as he brought from Quebec'; and 'his coat was French' (*TOMH*, 397-8). A bleeding nose completes the figure of 'abjection' that Orlando cuts on his return. He is abject both in the sense of being debased and degraded but also in the Kristevan sense of being confronted with the border between life and death.[10] Although he amends his appearance, Orlando's return is marked by the fact that he is not recognized, and in those he meets he arouses sensations both of abjection and the 'uncanny': he looks like Orlando but Orlando is known to be dead. Orlando's reception as a spectre sets the tone for the Gothicized final volume. It also simply amplifies the questions about his identity that are established at the outset of the novel.

THE TRIUMPH OF IDLENESS

Just as Smith collapses some of the differences between the chaste Monimia and the flighty Betsy Richards, so she draws attention to the proximity of Philip and Orlando Somerive. On numerous occasions, Philip playfully offers to be Orlando's 'double'. While Orlando does not lead the profligate lifestyle of his brother, he similarly organizes his life on the basis of his claim to the Rayland estate. Philip falls dramatically into debt, squanders the family estate, and lurches between Fleet Prison and the squalor of a London attic room, before succumbing to a fatal illness 'brought on by debauchery and excess' (*TOMH*, 505). Orlando is sexually continent and free from debt but is hardly a model of prudence and industry. He rejects his uncle Woodford's proposals to become a wine merchant in London and, before settling on a military commission, his plans for subsistence extend to availing himself of the 'rapid fortunes' to be made in India (though he 'had never considered, or perhaps heard the means by which they were acquired' (*TOMH*, 161)). His military career fails to bring him independence, financial or otherwise, so he plans to sell his commission for 'between three and four hundred pounds' and 'by dint of perseverance and industry, find some reputable employment, by which he might not only be enabled to assist his mother, but to keep a wife' (*TOMH*, 438). The only employment he undertakes, however, is pursuit of the lost will and when his fortune is reduced to 'two hundred and fifty pounds' he gives up his plan of further industry and trusts 'to Providence for the rest' (*TOMH*, 449). Orlando is eventually reduced to his last £30. Although he knows that the survival of his mother, his sisters and Monimia depend on 'his exertions' he is no closer to knowing 'what way of life to enter, or where to seek the means of providing for them' (*TOMH*, 507). Meanwhile, the 'dependent' Monimia discreetly finds 'constant employment' as a seamstress: 'Orlando saw her always busy; but he made no remarks on what occupied her; and without shocking his tenderness or his pride, she was thus enabled to add a little to the slender stock on which depended their subsistence' (*TOMH*, 487).

One possibility of employment does present itself to Orlando: 'the trade of authorship' (*TOMH*, 498). His talent as a poet is recognized by his friend Carr, though, in a sign of his lack of real promise for the rigours of professional authorship, Orlando is 'too idle to copy' one of his poems for him and gives him the original. The 'lost will' for which Orlando circuitously searches on his return from America signals, then, both a missing legal document and his uncertainty of purpose.

The eventual succession of Rayland Hall to Orlando Somerive is on the surface a sign that order has been restored; property has been retained within the family (an essential part in Britain's national security for Burke), the Somerive family home, West Wolverton, is returned to Orlando's family, and Monimia provides an heir to ensure the continuity of the Rayland name (now purchased by Orlando), its property and political authority. The means by which Orlando comes into his fortune, first by dint of the favouritism of his ancient aunt, then by the conscience of her erstwhile housekeeper, Lennard, who reveals the location of the hidden will, exposes the tenuous and vulnerable basis of his inheritance. Smith draws attention to the romantic nature of the discovery when she has Orlando reflect on its resemblance to a scene 'in old romances and fairy tales, where the hero is by some supernatural means directed to a golden key, which opens an invisible drawer, where a hand or an head is found swimming in blood' (*TOMH*, 518).

Property eventually overwhelms ability in this novel, but it is clear that the propertied have no greater moral claim to political representation than the able, that Betsy Richards would be as fit an heir to Rayland Hall as Orlando Somerive (evidenced in the ascension of her social equivalent, Monimia). It was as men of ability that the founders of the newly liberated America constructed their image. In 1793, as Burke's worst nightmare unfolded in France, as ability overwhelmed property, Smith's novel should have been a less comforting read than it evidently was for her romance-fixated readers, who noted only the triumph of old money and not the incursions of the new.

4

Double Vision and *The Emigrants*

Writing to her regular correspondent, the Irish antiquarian Joseph Cooper Walker in February 1793, Charlotte Smith describes her current literary enterprise: a poem in blank verse, in two parts, expected for publication in May of the same year, on the subject of the French emigrants – largely aristocracy, members of the middle classes and clergy – who were driven out of France for not adhering to the tenets of the new revolutionary regime and who arrived on the south coast of England in the early years of the 1790s. 'It is not a party book', she writes, 'but a conciliatory book.'[1] She does not expand on the nature of the conciliation offered or proposed in the poem in question, *The Emigrants*.[2] Given that she writes to Cooper in the month that war was declared between England and France and the poem is temporally poised on either side of this moment (November 1792, April 1793), she most obviously seems to be asking for conciliation between the two nations. The dedication to the poet William Cowper written in May 1793 amplifies this point. Appealing to Cowper's philanthropy, she hopes he will join her in hoping that:

> this painful exile may finally lead to the extirpation of that reciprocal hatred so unworthy of great and enlightened nations; that it may tend to humanize both countries, by convincing each, that good qualities exist in the other; and at length annihilate the prejudices that have so long existed to the injury of both. (Curran, 133)

This humanist agenda is certainly borne out at one level of the poem, which invites enlightened British readers to sympathize with their French 'brethren'. However, the poem is embedded with more subtle conciliations and contests: not only between

French and British, but also between royalists and revolutionaries, aristocrats and peasants, past and present, land and sea. Smith's speaker, perched on the cliffs or on the Downs may not be of 'a party' but neither is she entirely conciliatory, as she launches attacks on the British legal system and political corruption as though casting stones into the English Channel.

AMBIGUOUS SYMPATHY

To write about the plight of the emigrants here, and in her 1794 novel *The Banished Man*, signalled to Smith's less supportive critics a u-turn in her political sympathies. Thomas Lowes, a former friend who had become estranged from Smith when she took a 'democratic twist' in the early 1790s, saw her sympathy for the French émigrés as a symptom of the marriage of her daughter Anna Augusta to a French nobleman: 'not long after this', he snipes, 'her style both in conversation and novels altered considerably.'[3] The view that sympathy for French emigrants is a turn away from revolutionary politics is understandable if we consider that the cause of the recusant priests was being championed by counter-revolutionaries like Edmund Burke and Hannah More. It was Burke who had brought the plight of the exiled clergy to public attention. His plea led to a series of subscription appeals on their behalf throughout Britain. Hannah More was moved by Burke's appeal and prompted by Charles Burney (also an acquaintance of Smith) to take some of the refugees into her Bath home and to lend her services to a campaign to raise money for the priests' relief fund.[4] More saw them as victims of a godless republic, but Smith's portrait is of human suffering at the hands of 'closet Murderers, whom we style Wise Politicians', victims of schemes prepared 'to keep Europe's wavering balance even' (*TE*, 2, ll.320–2). For Smith they are political refugees.

Smith not only encountered such emigrants, but in late 1792 offered some of them refuge in her own lodgings in Brighthelmstone (modern Brighton). Indeed, her letter to Cooper reveals how she wrote the poem while a number of emigrants, 'some of whom are very agreeable Men', kept her company in her 'small book room'. While apparently enjoying the company of her French guests, she also seems to have been distracted from her writing endeavours by the 'confusion of tongue' around her (Stanton, 62). The simultaneous tone of hospitality and hostility in Smith's description of her guests can also be detected in the voice of the speaker of the poem, who invites her readers to sympathize with the plight of the displaced figures that she encounters on the Brighton coast, but to criticize the culture of corruption and uneven privilege from which they originate. *The Emigrants* is ambiguous in its sympathy. It provides a double vision of connection with the suffering of the emigrants and disconnection from their cultural provenance, unity with the revolutionary cause and dislocation from the progress of the actual revolution. As I shall demonstrate, this double vision is thematized as the speaker focuses on moments of seeing, gazing, obscured sight and ambiguous signs.

In a less literal sense, the double vision perhaps owes something to her inspiration for the poem, William Cowper's *The Task*, which delicately articulates its author's ambivalence about human progress. It is not only Cowper's moral and political vision that inspired Smith, but the 'conversational' mode of the poem, and its 'giving to the most familiar objects dignity and effect' (Dedication, *TE*, 132). In Cowper's hands, sofas, time-pieces and gardens give rise to meditations on nature and art, slavery, and rural poverty. Professing herself to have felt a 'kind of enchantment' on reading *The Task*, Smith was led 'to attempt, in Blank Verse, a delineation of those interesting objects which happened to excite my attention' (Dedication, *TE*, 132).

REFLUENT TIDES

The refluent character of the poem's conversational style – formally echoing the thematic movement between unity and separation, conciliation and contest – is reworked in the movement of the sea in Book 1. The opening finds readers of Smith's sonnets in familiar territory: 'the cliffs to the eastward of... Brighthelmstone' in the gloom of a winter morning, or more precisely, 'a morning in November, 1792', just weeks after the September massacres and Robespierre's ascension to power.

The subject of the poem allows us to read its mood in political terms: for revolutionary sympathizers like Smith, late 1792 brought with it foreboding and despondency but residual hope. This mixture is projected by the speaker on to the scene from the cliffs, as the sun struggles to shed light on the

> troubled waves;
> Their foaming tops, as they approach the shore
> And the broad surf that never ceasing breaks
> On the innumerous pebbles, catch the beams
> Of the pale Sun, that with reluctance gives
> To this cold northern Isle, its shorten'd day.
>
> (*TE*, 1, ll.2–7)

The waves are 'troubled' but 'never ceasing' and manage to 'catch' the light from the reluctant sun: the sea is gloomy but resilient and resourceful. A little later, the variety of the sea's moods conveys the operation of a benign force:

> He who bids
> The wild wind lift them till they dash the clouds,
> And speaks to them in thunder; or whose breath,
> Low murmuring o'er the gently heaving tides'
>
> (*TE*, 1, ll.20–3)

A God who 'knows/If but a Sew-Mew falls' must mean to man 'Nothing but good'. The sea becomes a feminized and seductive backdrop to the speaker's imaginary place of solitary refuge, a 'lone Cottage, deep embower'd/In the green woods' (*TE*, 1, ll.43–4) from where she will

> Gain the high mound, and mark these waves remote
> (Lucid tho' distant), blushing with the rays
> Of the far-flaming Orb, that sinks beneath them
>
> (*TE*, 1, ll.52-4)

From the speaker's pastoral refuge the sea becomes the analogy for the speaker's (doomed) tenacity:

> Onward I labour; as the baffled wave,
> Which yon rough beach repulses, that returns
> With the next breath of wind, to fail again.
>
> (*TE*, 1, ll.71–3)

The sea shifts from being a sympathetic fallacy, through

which the speaker establishes mood through external description, to a boundary, a maker of exiles. Recalling an apparently specific but unspecified period of exile from England (which in an autobiographical reading would be Smith's period in Normandy during 1784-5, where she went with her husband to escape debtor's prison) the speaker recalls:

> how sad
> It is to look across the dim cold sea,
> That melancholy rolls its refluent tides
> Between us and the dear regretted land
> We call our own –
>
> (*TE*, 1, ll.157-61)

The sea is both boundary and point of contact, its 'refluent tides' moving between England and France. The melancholic conversation between the English exile and her home, conveyed by the sea messenger, is echoed in the poem in the story of a French emigrant who

> with swol'n and aching eyes,
> Fix'd on the grey horizon, since the dawn
> Solicitously watch'd the weekly sail
> From her dear native land
>
> (*TE*, 1, ll.216–19)

The speaker and the French emigrant are women looking in opposite directions across the English Channel at different moments in history and stand as points of connection between England and France. Like the English speaker, the French woman dreams of her home in better times. Tired of her sea-watch, she 'yields awhile/To kind forgetfulness, while Fancy brings,/In waking dreams, that native land again!' (*TE*, 1, ll.219–21). Smith brings the reverie of unity to a sharp conclusion as we learn the content of the French woman's dream: 'Versaille appears' (*TE*, 1, l.221). The woman is an aristocrat who dreams of 'painted galleries,/And rooms of regal splendour; rich with gold' (*TE*, 1, ll.222–3). When she is roused from the 'gay visionary pageant' to 'drear reality' the sea before her is no longer a benign, conciliatory messenger. Rather, her cliffside hollow is encroached by 'dark'ning waves,/Urg'd by the rising wind, unheeded foam' (*TE*, 1, ll.230-1). Her dream of opulence dissolves in sea water.

This contest between the cultural privilege of the woman's past and the vulnerability of her present status, at the mercy of a nature that is figured in the threatening sea, is reworked in relation to another exile, presumably the woman's husband. A less sympathetic figure than his wife, he is figured as one, 'who long/Has dwelt amid the artifical scenes/Of populous city' and 'forgets all taste/For Nature's genuine beauty' (*TE*, 1, ll.260–5). The index of his insensitivity is his lack of appreciation for another stretch of water, an idealized ocean:

> in the lapse
> Of gushing waters [he] hears no soothing sound,
> . . . .
> Nor gazes pleas'd on Ocean's silver breast,
> While lightly o'er it sails the summer clouds
> Reflected in the wave, that, hardly heard,
> Flows on the yellow sands:
>
> (*TE*, 1, ll.265–6; 270–3)

The subtle pleasures of this placid ocean cannot compete with the noble's predilection for 'splendid shows,/The theatre, and pageant pomp of Courts'(*TE*, 1, ll.262–4).

The oscillation between the sea as conciliatory and contesting, between a benign and threatening natural force, is rehearsed again in the final two images of the sea in Book 1. The penultimate image comes as part of the speaker's warning to 'the pamper'd parasites' of the British government to heed the warning of the French revolution, 'that if oppress'd too long,/The raging multitude, to madness stung,/Will turn on their oppressors' (*TE*, 1, ll.333-5). The imagined British revolution is figured as a 'resistless torrent' in which 'Not only all your pomp may disappear,/But, in the tempest lost, fair Order sink/Her decent head' (*TE*, 1, ll.338-40). As the speaker's anger and the tempest subside, the benign sea reappears in an appeal to English humanity:

> English hearts,
> Of just compassion ever own the sway,
> As truly as our element, the deep,
> Obeys the mild dominion of the Moon. –
>
> (*TE*, 1, ll.360-3)

EXILE AND IDENTIFICATION

What I have called up to now oscillations, consciously designed movements between images of the sea as a gloomy portent and a benign force of natural or divine beauty, and a revolutionary tempest, are also erratic and at times contradictory. The clash of sea imagery is resonant of the broader inconsistency of Book 1 that shifts, not always comfortably, between the speaker's personal dejection and her compassion for and critique of the five emigrants she encounters. The speaker's identity, it seems, is fractured, dislocated and deracinated.

Unlike the speakers of the sonnets, who find only signs of their own isolation and extraordinary grief in the subjects of their poetry, the speaker of *The Emigrants* does identify with her subjects. The 'I' who enters the poem on line 42 is searching for a pastoral retreat from 'proud oppression and legal crimes' (*TE*, 1, l.36), but knows that no such place exists. No mortal home provides refuge from

> the spectre Care
> That from the dawn of reason, follows still
> Unhappy Mortals, 'till the friendly grave
> (Our sole secure asylum) 'ends the chace.'
>
> (*TE*, 1, ll.90–3)

The quotation on line 93 is noted as a debt to Edward Young, and it re-establishes her connection to the poets of melancholy that she secured with her sonnets. The 'sole secure asylum' of the grave is the resting place for Smith's speaker after she rejects a litany of other refuges: 'the Cot sequester'd' (*TE*, 1, l.75); the 'more substantial farm, well fenced and warm' (*TE*, 1, l.78); the 'statelier dome' of 'manorial residence' (*TE*, 1, l.80; l.86); the 'buildings, new and trim/With windows circling towards the restless Sea,/...ranged in rows'(*TE*, 1, ll.87–89) (the new Georgian terraces of 1790s Brighton). The homes of the peasant, the farmer, the gentry and the new middle class, which might be figured in more traditionally patriotic terms as the domestic fortresses of the freeborn Englishman are, in Smith's hands, haunted houses; they are private spaces rendered 'uncanny' by the 'Care' of public life. The uncanny character of the Sussex homes, that is their strangeness, their unfamiliarity, their 'unhomeliness', anticipates the speaker's description of the itinerant French, whose home, 'their distracted Country' (*TE*, 1, l.98) is divided against itself. The speaker looks on them first with compassion and her apostrophe, 'Behold', invites readers to do the same. They are 'Sad heralds of distress!' whose 'dejected looks':

>   proclaim them Men
> Banish'd for ever and for conscience sake
> From their distracted Country, whence the name
> Of Freedom misapplied, and much abus'd
> By lawless Anarchy, has driven them far
> To wander;
>
> <div align="right">(<i>TE</i>, 1, ll.96–101)</div>

Immediately, however, the speaker introduces a dissonant note when we learn that they wander 'with the prejudice they learn'd/ From Bigotry (the Tut'ress of the blind),/Thro' the wide World unshelter'd' (*TE*, 1, ll.101–3).

The speaker spares little time before cataloguing the 'errors' of the exiles that helped to precipitate the Revolution. She begins with the clergy; so 'droops one,/Who in a moping cloister long consum'd/This life inactive, to obtain a better' (*TE*, 1, ll.113–15), guilty of cloistered virtue; 'Another, of more haughty port'(*TE*, 1, l.125) dwells on 'all he lost – the Gothic dome,/That vied with splendid palaces (*TE*, 1, ll.128–9) and ambitions of becoming another 'Fleuri, Richlieu, Alberoni' (*TE*, 1, l.141), who were men of great political as well as clerical power in France. She finds a more sympathetic tone for the parochial priest, who knew none of the trappings of power and who tended to his peasant clergy, but who finds himself an exile from the new Republic. The speaker invites our sympathy, then, for their banishment and disdain for their (Catholic) prejudice and appeals to the 'enlightened' English (Protestant) sensibilities of her readers when she asks them to put aside their prejudices and welcome 'These ill'starr'd Exiles' who:

>   now seek
> In England an asylum – well deserve
> To find that (every prejudice forgot,
> Which pride and ignorance teaches), we for them
> Feel as our brethren;
>
> <div align="right">(<i>TE</i>, 1, ll.356–60)</div>

EXILE AND MOTHERHOOD

The point of connection between the emigrants and Smith's speaker is figured as a 'mournful truth' to which the emigrants bear witness: the condition of homelessness, or, at least, the sense that no home is a refuge. It is connection in dislocation. As discussed above, the speaker knows the condition of exile, her 'Involuntary exile' away from England (*TE*, 1, l.156) and, implicitly, in England itself. Her longing for home was at a time 'while yet/England had charms for me' (*TE*, 1, ll.156–7). Implicitly, England has now lost its charm; the speaker is now exiled at home.

The distance between the speaker's happier past and a melancholy present is recast in the plight of the French woman nestled in a hollow in the cliffside. Before she is revealed as an aristocrat, she is presented as a mother, whose children play at her feet. The children make paper boats to launch a 'mimic navy' (*TE*, 1, l.210), an image that poignantly reduces military power to a plaything. There are, then, two points of contact between Smith's speaker and the dreaming woman. The first is exile, literalized in their postures as they gaze out to sea (the speaker in the past looking from France to England, the woman in the present looking from England to France), both looking for signs of life from home. The second is motherhood. The speaker and the author foreground their own maternal status in Book 2, with a reference to Smith's litigation battles over her children's trust fund. Having tried to recall a time when the arrival of May would herald 'gay delight' (*TE*, 2, l.326) she reflects with horror on the fact that now the 'bright Sun of that delicious month' awakens her to 'never-ending toil':

> To terror and to tears! – Attempting still,
> With feeble hands and cold desponding heart,
> To save my children from the o'erwhelming wrongs,
> That have for ten long years been heap'd on me!
>
> (*TE*, 2, ll.351–4)

The image of the martyr mother is revisited when the speaker looks forward to her death: looks forward both in the sense of looking to the future and anticipating with pleasure. She imagines 'the little praise, that may await/The Mother's efforts'

(*TE*, 2, ll.380–1) once she is in the grave and asks an addressee to 'vindicate my humble fame; to say/That, not in selfish sufferings absorb'd,/"I gave to misery all I had, my tears"' (*TE*, 2, ll.383–5). The reference to Gray's 'Elegy Written in a Country Church-Yard' (from the poet's epitaph: 'He gave to misery all he had, a tear') both recalls Smith's *Elegiac Sonnets* and marks Smith's speaker out from Gray's and the sonneteer as less self-absorbed, devoted to the well-being of her children.

Images of motherhood recur throughout Book 2. Marie Antoinette is figured in an abject state of motherhood, divided from her own feelings as she looks upon her son, the imprisoned heir Louis: 'Thy wretched Mother, petrified with grief,/Views thee with stony eyes, and cannot weep!' (*TE*, 2, ll.152-3). Another 'wretched' mother appears in a 'melancholy tale' recounted to the speaker by one of the exiles. The story is of a French family torn apart by war. The mother, having fled from hostile troops, seeks shelter in the mountains:

> – clasping close
> To her hard-heaving heart her sleeping child,
> All she could rescue of the innocent groupe [sic]
> That yesterday surrounded her.
>
> (*TE*, 2, ll.264-7)

She is caught between life and death, wishing she 'had staid/To die with those affrighted Fancy paints/The lawless soldier's victims' (*TE*, 2, ll.270-2), but 'in death itself/True to maternal tenderness' she wants to 'protect/This last dear object of her ruin'd hopes' (*TE*, 2, ll.279-80; ll.284-5). The death of mother and child prepare the way for the tragic denouement of the tale: the return from battle of 'the feudal Chief' to a devastated home:

> by the blunted light
> That the dim moon thro'painted casements lends,
> He sees that devastation has been there:
>
> (*TE*, 2, ll.300-3)

The dreadful clarity of the scene before him, despite the 'blunted light', is a play on the aesthetic of the sublime, a much-used effect of Gothic fiction. His mind and body have a separate experience of the horror: 'while each hideous image to his mind/Rises terrific, o'er a bleeding corse/Stumbling he falls'(*TE*, 2, ll.303-4): the image before his mind has a life of its own; the body at his feet is lifeless. This self-division is complete when

> the day dawns
> On a wild and raving Maniac, whom a fate
> So sudden and calamitous has robb'd
> Of reason;
>
> (*TE*, 2, ll.308–11)

VISION AND SPECTACLE

It is characteristic of Book 2 that 'he *sees* the devastation' (my emphasis) and it is the 'hideous *image*' of his family's death that robs the father of his reason. Throughout *The Emigrants*, vision has peculiar significance. In Book 1, sight is conveyed through relatively neutral verbs such as looking, gazing or simply seeing. Sight is often disturbed by tears, for example, 'with swol'n and aching eyes' (*TE*, 1, l.216) and 'With tearful eyes and heaving bosoms' (*TE*, 1, l.229). There *are* visions in Book 1, that is, images of the mind not the eyes, and these are usually of happier times or favoured places contrasted with the dreary reality of the present scene. In Book 2, sight and vision are heightened and horrific. Eyes are not only 'swol'n' with grief but 'swimming', unable to take in the scenes before them (*TE*, 2, ll.46). Scenes become 'spectacles' (*TE*, 2, l.56). That is not to say that vision in Book 1 is twenty-twenty. There is much emphasis on ways of seeing that distort value. So the aristocratic couple who 'see not the simple dignity of Virtue' (*TE*, 1, l.257)

> *Their* eyes,
> Accustom'd to regard the splendid trophies
> Of Heraldry (that with fantastic hand
> Mingles, like images in feverish dreams,
> 'Gorgons and Hydras, and Chimeras dire,'
> With painted puns and visionary shapes;)
>
> (*TE*, 1, ll.251–6)

Milton's Gorgons, Hydras and Chimeras, his abominations of nature, are here equivalent to the artifice of French aristocracy in whose world despotism 'hides/His features harsh, beneath the diadem/Of worldly grandeur' (*TE*, 1, ll.274–6).

If the exiled nobles of Book 1 must learn to see 'the simple dignity of Virtue' (*TE*, 1, l.258), the people of Britain will learn to see through the 'parading forms' (*TE*, 1, 1.336) of their oppressors, the 'pamper'd Parasites' (*TE*, 1, 1.330) of the British government. Just as Burke had prophesied the revolutionary events in France, so Smith offers her own prophecy of revolution in England, as the fraudulent signs of power – 'sounding titles and parading forms' (*TE*, 1, l.337) – are stripped away by those in their thrall. Smith ends her first volume on a pacific note, with the hope that the spirit of sympathy and compassion with which the emigrants have been received in England is the spirit in which the longstanding enmity between the two nations will be resolved:

> – Actions such as these,
> Like incense rising to the Throne of Heaven,
> Far better justify the pride, that swells
> In British bosoms, than the deafening roar
> Of Victory from a thousand brazen throats,
>
> (*TE*, 1, ll.376–80)

The humanist call for peace, then, is based on the model of sympathy between the English hosts and the French emigrants. The conciliatory vision of Book 1, however, is embedded with a revolutionary vision of a British mob turning on their oppressors.

WAR AND PEACE

Smith silently concedes the futility of her hope for peace when she opens her second volume on an afternoon in April 1793, looking across the sea from 'an Eminence on one of those Downs, which afford to the South a View of the Sea' (*TE*, 2, 149), a view which might well afford glimpses of naval ships, as war was declared between England and France in February of that year, weeks after the execution of Louis XVI. In Book 2, then, the speaker retreats from her liminal place on the cliffs to a safer place inland and landscape takes the place of sea as the index of the speaker's state of mind and the state of the world outside. The sea is now invoked both as a protective barrier ('this seafenc'd isle' (*TE*, 2, l.65); 'by the rude sea guarded we are safe,/ And feel not evils such as with deep sighs/The Emigrants deplore' (*TE*, 2, ll.210–12)) and a distant marker of the horizon ('till the Sun/Sinks in the rosy waters of the West' (*TE*, 2, ll.183–4)).

It is not the effects of revolution that dominate Book 2, but the effects of war. The opening view of the springtime landscape is darkened both by the speaker's dejection and by the prospect of hostilities with France. The evocation of spring emphasises the uncertainty of the moment in which the blooms appear:

> here I mark Spring's humid hand unfold
> The early leaves that fear capricious winds,
> While, even on sheltered banks, the timid flowers
> Give, half reluctantly, their warmer hues
> To mingle with the primroses' pale stars.
>
> (*TE*, 2, ll.23–7)

The latent threat to the spring blooms, 'even on sheltered banks', mirrors the fragility of peace in 'this sea-fenc'd isle' (*TE*, 2, l.65), or at least the impossibility of hope in its season while 'in neighbouring countries' unfold 'scenes that make the sick heart shudder' (*TE*, 2, ll.66–7). In France the rural peace is disturbed by 'the trumpet's voice' of war (*TE*, 2, l.68), the 'violets...are stain'd with blood' (*TE*, 2, l.70–1), and 'thy lilies, [are] trampled now in dust,/And blood-bespotted' (*TE*, 2, ll.105–6). But the contrast between the English and French landscapes is not only between images of fragile security and the effects of full-blown military hostilities. The English landscape, though not disturbed by 'hostile hoof...nor fierce flames' (*TE*, 2, l.207) is 'too oft deformed/By figures' (*TE*, 2, ll.204–5) who live in 'extremest poverty' (*TE*, 2, l.190). This reference to the poor of England revives the revolutionary overtones of Book 1. They are present, too, in an image of the French Prince Louis. In a pastoral interlude the speaker addresses the prince and wishes that:

> in an humble sphere, perhaps content:
> Thou hadst been free and joyous on the heights
> Of Pyrennean mountains, shagg'd with woods
> Of chestnut, pine and oak: as on those hills
> Is yonder little thoughtless shepherd lad,
>
> . . . .
>
> While, half forgetful of his simple task,
> Hardly his length'ning shadow, or the bells'

> Slow tinkling of his flock
> . . . .
> Recall the happy idler.
>
> (*TE*, 2, ll.132–6; 140–2; 145)

Concealed within the wish of 'Pyrennean' pastoral bliss for the unfortunate dauphin is a republican vision of the prince become peasant.

DESIRE AND DISLOCATION

The pastoral wish for the prince is recalled in the speaker's desires for herself. When the speaker's despondency is reintroduced as a topic she wishes she could return to her infancy when she had no 'thoughts like these' (*TE*, 2, l.325). She calls for 'Memory' to come:

> And from distracting cares, that now deprive
> Such scenes of all their beauty, kindly bear
> My fancy to those hours of simple joy,
> When, on the banks of Arun, which I see
> Make its irriguous course thro yonder meads,
> I play'd;
>
> (*TE*, 2, ll.330–5)

This vision of the past involves the river not the sea. The river's welcoming domesticity is emphasized in the speaker's memory of how she 'meditated how to venture best/Into the shallow current' (*TE*, 2, ll.338–9). Such unity is harder to come by for the adult speaker, and when it comes it is with the changeable sea as she offers a prayer for peace:

> – I made my prayer
> In unison with murmuring waves that now
> Swell with dark tempests, now are mild and blue,
> As the bright arch above;
>
> (*TE*, 2, ll.401–3)

A prayer made in unison with a capricious sea is not resounding in its confidence, and echoes the volatility that Smith describes towards the end of Book 2, as God's 'creatures' tear the 'bleeding breast' of the 'suffering globe' and Man 'Himself a worm, desire[s] unbounded rule/O'er beings like himself' (*TE*, 2, ll.425–6).

When she wrote to Cooper at the time of composing her 'conciliatory book', Smith was surrounded by the emigrants of whose plight she writes, as she opened her Brighton home as a refuge. In typically ambivalent fashion, Smith alludes both to the pleasure afforded by the 'company...[of] very agreeable men' and to the 'confusion of tongue' that arises from their presence 'and prevents my adding more' to her letter to Cooper (Stanton, 62). Given that Smith's correspondence is littered with references to the circumstances that hinder her writing – either professional or personal – this is not a surprising comment. But it does underline the fluent and refluent character of the poem, as it tries to accommodate sympathy for the émigrés and a critique of the system that produced them. It is a viewpoint that requires double vision and demands an uncomfortable fracturing of subjectivity for the poem's speaker. The dislocated self of the *Elegiac Sonnets* resurfaces.

5

Mourning Complete?: *Beachy Head*

Beachy Head is the end of a journey.[1] It is one of a collection of posthumously published poems by Smith and composition began around 1803, although her correspondence suggests that it underwent revision until just before her death in 1806.[2] The eponymous landmark signals the end of the literal journey taken by travellers between France and England, a journey that Smith figuratively made throughout her writing career. The poem is arguably the least autobiographical of any of her work. There is a brief reference to her 'guiltless exile' (*BH*, l.288) from 'these upland solitudes' (*BH*, l.283), the author's move from Sussex to London, but the poem does not have the sustained, albeit mediated, self-referentiality of the *Sonnets* or *The Emigrants*. There are echoes of the historical voice of Helen Maria Williams, that as we will see moves between the grand narrative voice of historians like Robertson and the moral, arbitrating voice of female historians like Macauley. As Theresa Kelley has persuasively argued in her reading of *Beachy Head*, Smith grafts together two historical models: the first a classical, linear model, focusing on 'politics and statecraft' (reminiscent of the histories of Gibbon, Robertson and Hume); the second focusing on 'personal experience, eyewitness accounts, and even spectatorial sympathy [that] disrupted the protocols of classical historiography'.[3] She welds together the 'prospect' view of the male historian and what Marx would call 'history from below'. She does not do so seamlessly, however, and the gaps between the narrative voices, the clash of historicist discourses, her tendency to engage with and then abandon different kinds of knowledge, are the most striking and perplexing aspects of the poem.

Although there is less of 'Smith the author' in this poem than in her earlier work, the poem's location, on Beachy Head, obviously summons up the landscape of the author's childhood on which she dwells in such a melancholy fashion throughout the *Elegiac Sonnets*. Here, Beachy Head and the Sussex landscape stand for more than the author's history, however. The history embedded beneath the 'stupendous summit' of this 'rock sublime' is biblical, global, national, domestic and minutely local.

HISTORICAL BREAKDOWN

The attempt to hold all these histories together breaks down in a series of formal and thematic splits and dissonances throughout the poem. The first series of rifts in the poem happens after four lines:

> I would recline; while Fancy should go forth,
> And represent the strange and awful hour
> Of vast concussion; when the Omnipotent
> Stretch'd forth his arm,
> . . . .
>   and from the continent
> Eternally divided this green isle.
>
>   (*BH*, ll.4–7; 9–10)

The speaker who 'would recline' on the summit of Beachy Head at daybreak splits from 'Fancy', who 'should go forth' to represent the moment when France and Britain were rendered geologically separate. 'Fancy' is 'fancied' going to engage with the grand sweep of an uncertain history. It is uncertain because embedded in the 'vast concussion' that separates Britain from the rest of Europe is a tension between biblical explanation (the 'Omnipotent...arm') and an emerging geological understanding of the shape of the landscape, to which the poem returns later. The reclining 'I', meanwhile, is absorbed in the details of present day, from the light show of the sunrise, to the birds nesting in the cliffside, the shepherd rounding up his sheep, and the changing light of sunset.

The speaker's eye is caught by a fleet of fishing boats and further on the horizon 'a dubious spot', a commercial ship bound for India to collect the spoils of Britain's growing imperial trade. The diamonds and pearls which make up the plunder are the 'toys of Nature' (*BH*, 1.55) and are 'of little estimate in Reason's eye' (*BH*, 1.56). Their beauty is 'poor and paltry' compared to 'the lovely light' of the stars, the moon and the setting sun (*BH*, 1.71). While Fancy 'should' be exploring the origins of Britain's split from Europe, it is found, distracted, mid-way through this section as it 'fondly soars,/Wandering sublime thro' visionary vales' in the sky (*BH*, 1.86). The beauty of the present scene places more insistent demands on the attention of Reason and Fancy than does its natural history or its commercial associations.

This finely calibrated evaluation of the worth of things continues throughout *Beachy Head* as at times the speaker, at times a personified abstraction (Reason, Fancy, Contemplation, Memory) look on the scene from their different perspectives, a difference made 'literal' from their slightly different situations on the promontory. So, 'Contemplation, here,/High on her throne of rock' bids 'recording Memory unfold/Her scroll voluminous' (*BH*, ll.117–20) and look back to the Norman invasion of this shoreline. It is a history so 'grand' that the narrative cannot be contained in the verse, however, and the details spill over into an extensive note, in a pattern that is repeated throughout *Beachy Head*. The notes themselves are often querulous, as though the author cannot decide whether they add to or diminish the authority of her verse. The most telling example is a note on fossil shells which the speaker 'in fancy still' observes, 'objects more minute.../... the strange and foreign forms/Of sea-shells' in the chalk hills (*BH*, ll.368–74):

> Among the crumbling chalk I have often found shells, some quite in a fossil state and hardly distinguishable from chalk.... It is now many years since I made these observations. The appearance of sea-shells so far from the sea excited my surprise, though I then knew nothing of natural history. I have never read any of the late theories of the earth, nor was I ever satisfied with the attempts to explain many of the phenomena which call forth conjecture in those books I happened to have had access to on this subject. (*BH*, 232)

The note draws attention to the conflicting discourses within the emergent science of geology, discourses which range from theology to travelogue and with which Smith, paradoxically, declares impatience and ignorance. More questions than answers about the origins of the fossils pile up in the verse, until the speaker dismisses the enquiry altogether, to focus instead on the daily grind of the peasant:

> Ah! Very vain is Science' [sic] proudest boast,
> And but a little light its flame yet lends
> To its most ardent votaries; since from whence
> These fossil forms are seen, is but conjecture,
> Food for vague theories, or vain dispute,
> While to his daily task the peasant goes,
> Unheeding such inquiry;
>
> (*BH*, ll.390–6)

GEORGIC VIEWS

Thus far, Smith has launched a series of authoritative discourses only to withdraw from them: she finds it impossible to contain national history within her verse, recasts the language of colonial exploration as hollow commercial exploitation, and dismisses nascent geological enquiry as 'conjecture', a branch of 'vain' Science. These 'prospect' views which claim broad geographical and historical vision seem to be supplanted in the poem by a view close to the ground, though not 'from below'. The peasant 'unheeding' of scientific enquiry has his eyes on 'the earth he cultivates' (*BH*, l.398) and:

> As little recks [knows] the herdsman of the hill,
> Who on some turfy knoll, idly reclined,
> . . . .
>   that deep beneath
> Rest the remains of men, of whom is left
> No traces in the records of mankind,
>
> (*BH*, ll.399–403)

The privileged view seems to be the Georgic's: the tiller of the land, the shepherd, 'the hind/Who, with his own hands rears on some black moor' (*BH*, l.194) who attend to what is before their eyes. But the happiness of the Georgic's 'unreflecting' vision, the 'simple scenes of peace and industry', which are so appealing to the 'reflecting mind' (*BH*, ll.167–8) is undercut by the knowledge that the shepherd quits his 'more honest toil' for 'Clandestine traffic' (*BH*, l.183), smuggling. The smugglers are implicitly encouraged by the scarcity of agricultural production: 'fields that shew/As angry Heaven had rain'd sterility,/Stony and cold, and hostile to the plough' (ll.229–31). This agricultural scarcity is formally associated with war by the previous line's reference to the appearance of 'hostile war-fires flashing to the sky' (*BH*, l.228).

Perhaps the more privileged view is not of the labourer, however unreflecting his happiness, but the 'recliner'. The poem, as we have seen already, is populated by 'reclining figures' intent on the view before them: the speaker who watches the changing light of day; the 'herdsman of the hill,/ Who on some turfy knoll, idly reclined,/Watches his wether flock' (*BH*, ll.399–400); '[s]ome pensive lover of uncultur'd flowers' who 'reclines' among 'o'ershadowing woods of beech' (*BH*, ll.355–9). The 'lover of uncultur'd flowers' is a figure from the speaker's childhood memory, discovered as she worshipped at 'Nature's shrine' (*BH*, l.346) (a line reminiscent of Wordsworth's *Tintern Abbey*).[4] The gaze of this recliner is on the flora and fauna of the shaded undergrowth. Like the speaker, the figure takes pleasure in the name, the anatomy and figurative potential of the plants: they are both enthusiastic botanists.

Botany was, by the late eighteenth century, a popular scientific pursuit, especially for genteel women, and Smith used her extensive botanical knowledge in a range of texts.[5] It is tempting to find in botany the antidote to the grand narratives with which Smith's speaker engages but ultimately dismisses in the poem. It is, after all, the science of the local, the minute, open to the eye but requiring a downward gaze; and finally, it is a science pursued by women. However, botany partly became so popular not because of its domestic potential but because of the exotic species that were imported from around the globe on geographical expeditions. The imperial plantation of tea and sugar-cane was partly developed on the back of botanical gardens in Britain like Kew where crop systems could be tested. The species under the botanical gaze of this poem are native to Britain and most are named in a section in which the speaker remembers her Sussex childhood. The speaker luxuriates in the common names of the plants ('woodbine', tangling 'vetch', 'bittersweet' and 'bryony' (*BH*, ll.350–2)) while the author glosses the Latin in simple notes. Predictably, Smith's use of botany takes a more argumentative turn when, in the next heavily annotated section on plants, the notes give a flavour of contemporary botanical dispute. So, she writes, Linaeus was mistaken in his identification of flowers that mimic insects as 'forming one species' and a Thomas Martyn is cited arguing with other botanists who claim that sheep that eat aromatic plants yield a superior flavour of mutton. 'The truth is' he is quoted as saying 'that sheep do not crop on these aromatic plants' (*BH*, 236).

It is arguable whether such references display Smith's botanical authority, alert as she is to the detail of contemporaneous debate, or are there to display the limits of human understanding. This uncertainty characterizes the poem. The speaker introduces a way of seeing the world (national history; imperial narrative; geological excavation; botany) only to recoil, settle for the 'unreflecting' gaze of the peasant, the herdsman, the shepherd. Imvariably the 'lowly' gaze is found wanting and the speaker revives the historical or scientific authority. For instance, beneath the 'herdsman of the hill', whose vision had seemed to supplant science, lies what the herdsman does not see:

> the remains of men, of whom is left
> No traces in the records of mankind,
> Save what these half obliterated mounds
> And half fill'd trenches doubtfully impart
> To some lone antiquary;

(*BH*, ll.402–6)

As though she cannot stop herself, the speaker recounts what the 'lone antiquary' 'loves to contemplate': two thousand years of history embedded in the hill. His 'fancy' leads him to the relics of Roman emperors and to consider

> What time the huge unwieldy Elephant
> Auxiliary reluctant, hither led,
> From Afric's forest glooms and tawny sands,
> First felt the Northern blast, and his vast frame
> Sunk useless;

(*BH*, ll.412–17)

A digressive note gives the speculative history of the fragments of an elephant discovered in Burton Park in 1740. The authorial fascination with the details of this archeological discovery clashes dissonantly with the image of the elephant sinking 'useless', an image picked up by the speaker as she invokes:

> Hither, Ambition come!
> Come and behold the nothingness of all
> For which you carry thro' the oppressed Earth,
> War, and its train of horrors –
>
> (*BH*, ll.419–22)

The futility of the Romans bringing an elephant to Britain and the fascination of the 'wondering hinds' who 'on those enormous bones/Gaz'd' (*BH*, ll.415–16) crystallizes the split in the poem between the compelling character of sublime human endeavour (historical, scientific, mythic), and the futility and 'horrors' of its misapplication (warfare, empire).

SOCIABLE POSSIBILITIES

The reclining posture of the pastoral hind and the lowly gaze of the botanist may seem a refuge from such futile 'Ambition' and certainly would have been the refuge Smith advocated throughout her sonnets. However, glimpses of other more sociable possibilities are offered in *Beachy Head*. Just as the authorial notes, however argumentative or sceptical, suggest an engagement with the material that is otherwise abandoned in the verse, so there is an insistence in the poem on social engagement and a rhetoric of hope that was striking in its absence from the melancholic sonnets. For instance, the human eye may be limited in its range but, the poem suggests, there are things of value to see if you move your position:

> if the eye could reach so far, the mart
> Of England's capital, its domes and spires
> Might be perceived –
>
> (*BH*, ll.484–6)

Just as the eye cannot capture all of the available view so the poet cannot contain in verse all the available features, as Smith acknowledges: 'Description falls so infinitely short of the reality, that only here and there, distinct features can be given' (*BH*, 238). As the poem draws to its end Smith focuses in one of those features, a dismantled fortress now home to a 'tiller of the soil' (*BH*, l.500). The tiller's fortress home brings to mind a man who lived in such a 'castellated mansion once' (*BH*, l.506). This man, the first of two hermits whose lives feature at the end of *Beachy Head*, is the last recumbent figure of the poem: 'stretch'd upon the mountain turf/With folded arms, and eyes intently fix'd (*BH*, ll.522-3). Locals view him with suspicion and think 'His senses injur'd' (*BH*, l.520). Despite his complaints and murmurs, he is heard in song, imagining himself 'a Shepherd on the hill' (*BH*, l.531) and summoning the memory of a lost lover. This is not the melancholy wanderer of the *Sonnets*, however, as 'it seem'd as if young Hope/Her flattering pencil gave to Fancy's hand' (*BH*, ll.556-7). He vanishes but his presence is still felt in discovered 'love songs and scatter'd rhymes/Unfinish'd sentences, or half erased,/And rhapsodies' (*BH*, ll.574-6). He lives on, the speaker suggests, in the woods, but in his mind, he may have built another world:

> He, in some island of the southern sea,
> May haply build his cane-constructed bower
> Beneath the bread-fruit, or aspiring palm,
> With long green foliage rippling in the gale.

(*BH*, ll.663-6)

Characteristically, while the tenor of the verse is about the hope that he can cherish in his 'ideal bliss' (*BH*, l.667), the 'island of the southern sea' is glossed as 'the newly discovered islands' of Polynesia, 'where it was first believed men lived in a state of simplicity and happiness; but where, as later enquiries have ascertained, that exemption from toil...produces the grossest vices' (*BH*, 245). The recumbent life is ideal only in the ideal sense, it seems.

As the speaker turns back to Beachy Head itself, to a cavern in the cliff-face, a second recluse is introduced. He is identified in the notes as Parson Darby, 'who for many years had no other abode than this cave,' and 'had often administered assistance to ship-wrecked mariners' (*BH*, 245). He is figured here as 'one, who long disgusted with the world/And all its ways, appear'd to suffer life/Rather than live' (*BH*, ll.674-6). A man of sensibility 'feelingly alive to all that breath'd', he retreats from the world but rejoins it now and then to snatch 'From the wild billows, some unhappy man/Who liv'd to bless the hermit of the rocks' (*BH*, ll.707–9). Although he eventually succumbs to the sea, his death, and life, are represented as meaningful. That 'meaning' is left on the cliff-face:

> Those who read
> Chisel'd within the rock, these mournful lines,
> Memorials of his sufferings, did not grieve,
> That dying in the cause of charity
> His spirit, from its earthly bondage freed,
> Had to some better region fled for ever.
>
> (*BH*, ll.726–31)

There has been critical debate about the status of 'these mournful lines' to which the speaker refers.[6] As the poem was published posthumously, there is speculation that an intended epitaph was never completed, an idea corroborated by the prefatory advertisement written by the publisher which suggests that Smith had promised more material after delivering the manuscript in May 1806. The missing material, however, was thought by the publisher Johnson to be a preface.[7] Perhaps the 'meaning' lies less in the missing lines, or in the preceding 727 lines of poetry to which 'these mournful lines' may refer, than in 'the cause of charity' for which the hermit dies.

Smith's own last days were taken up with asking for 'charity' for her own children. Smith developed uterine or ovarian cancer and spent her last few years in great pain and remained preoccupied with securing her children's financial dues. Letters from Smith to the Earl of Egremont, who had been drafted in by William Hayley to deal with Smith's claim on the family trust, grew increasingly beseeching and at times hostile as his interest in her circumstances dwindled and her need for his support increased. Benjamin Smith died several months before Charlotte, finally releasing the money from her marriage settlements, which could be distributed amongst her surviving children.

The trust was settled some seven years after her death. By this time Smith's work had already drifted from public attention, although there are signs of her influence in the novels of Jane Austen and Charles Dickens and, of course, in Wordsworth's poetry. Wordsworth himself paid tribute to Smith in 1833, calling her 'a lady to whom English verse is under greater obligations than are likely to be acknowledged or remembered'.[8] A sustained process of acknowledgement and remembering has now been underway for two decades in the revival of critical interest in Smith's work, a revival that is helping to reshape the landscape of British Romanticism.

6

The Ties that Bind: Williams' Poetry of the 1780s

Adam Smith's view that 'the poets were the first historians' can be found in many eighteenth-century accounts of the 'evolution' of history writing.[1] Prose was generally understood to have succeeded poetry as a higher, more sophisticated form of history writing, emanating from societies that have 'progressed' to more complex stages of organization.[2] The historians of commercial, eighteenth-century Britain would, by such logic, write in prose not poetry. While history was understood to be formally evolving towards non-fictional prose, expectations about the effect of history writing on the reader left the distinction between historical and imaginative forms of writing blurred. Eighteenth-century history was expected to stimulate the reader's passions and sympathies as much as any work of fiction. When, in the advertisement to her 1784 poem, *Peru*, Helen Maria Williams explains that she is not presuming to attempt 'a full, historical narration of the fall of the Peruvian empire', only 'a simple detail of some few incidents that make a part of that romantic story',[3] she gestures to a tradition of writing which demands narrative flair of its historians:

> To describe that important event with accuracy, and to display with clearness and force the various causes which combined to produce it, would require all the energy of genius, and the most glowing colours of imagination. (*Poems*, 1786, 2, 53)

To write 'historical poetry' in the eighteenth century is to evoke an earlier historical moment when poets were the historians. The setting of Williams' poem is such a historical moment, and its subject is a society at a 'primitive' stage of civilization, whose 'innocent and amiable people, form the most affecting subjects of true pathos' and who inhabit an exotic climate, 'totally unlike our own'. The fallen empire of Peru is ripe for 'poetic description' (*Poems 1786*, 2, 54). The narration of the history of the Peruvian empire had recently been undertaken in prose by the French historian Guillaume Thomas Raynal (in his *Histoire philosophique des...deux Indes* (1770)) and by his Scottish 'rival' William Robertson in *The History of America* (1777). Williams draws on both of these sources in her account of the Spanish colonization of Peru. As I shall suggest, Williams evidently shares many of Robertson's assumptions about the benign state of British commerce and his cosmopolitanism, the ideal of a common civilization that he shared with many other 'enlightenment' historians.[4] Both Williams and Robertson project those values on to their reading of the failure of the Spanish imperial project in South America. There the similarity between their accounts ends. In his introduction to the Woodstock edition of Williams' poems, Jonathan Wordsworth finds the poem wanting in the historicity he finds in its source: 'Though Robertson's *History of America* is referred to in the notes, the stories of tyranny and love have almost nothing to do with historical fact...Everything depends on our response to the emotions of barely characterized pairs of lovers' (*Poems 1786*, 1, 4). Wordsworth seems to miss the point that *Peru* is a sentimental poem inspired by a historical account. But if we measure Williams' historical achievement alongside Robertson's and other eighteenth-century historians, we might find that the 'lack' of historical veracity in the poem is as much to do with the gendered perspective of its author as with generic convention. Robertson and other male historians of the eighteenth century claim what Karen O'Brien calls the social authority of the 'experienced and philosophically well-travelled adjudicator...of political causes and contests'. By virtue of the relative cultural marginality of all women in the eighteenth century, Williams shares with even the most celebrated of female historians, Catherine Macauley and Mercy Otis Warren, 'social authority...as the female bearers and arbitrators of moral standards'.[5] To foreground the emotional impact of historical events on fictionalized characters, as Williams does in her poetry, her fiction and her non-fictional prose, is to test out the morality and measure the ethical standards under which historical events were enacted.

EDWIN AND ELTRUDA

It is as an arbiter of moral standards, then, that Williams offers us her historical poetry of the 1780s. The poem she published first and composed at the age of nineteen, *Edwin and Eltruda: A Legendary Tale* (1782) is a ballad on the War of the Roses, inspired in part by the revival in interest in all things medieval at the end of the eighteenth century and by the kind of historical education available to middle-class girls like Williams.[6] As we have seen in the context of Smith's early poetry, the medieval revival found its expression in the writing of sonnets but also in the collection and publication of ancient tales, and the imitation of the old forms by a new generation of balladeers, who were much disparaged by contemporary reviewers. Ballads, which were originally songs transmitted orally, were transcribed or reinvented as a literary form in the late eighteenth century. The most celebrated example is Wordsworth and Coleridge's *Lyrical Ballads* (1798), narrative poems that imitated the style of the oral ballad. Wordsworth joined in the critique of other, less skilled balladeers when, in the Preface to *Lyrical Ballads*, he refers to 'deluges of idle stories in verse'. *Edwin and Eltruda* with its common ballad stanza, a quatrain with ac bd rhymes repeated throughout its 396 lines and heightened sentimental content, would no doubt, for Wordsworth, count as one of these hapless tales. It certainly lacks the self-conscious 'framing' of romance and sentiment that makes Smith's poetry more palatable to the tastes of her contemporaries. However, the poem is an instructive starting place to understand Williams' approach to history in poetry.

The historical backdrop for the poem is the intermittent civil war fought from 1455 to 1487 between the Houses of Lancaster and York, which originated in the disputed succession of the Lancastrian monarch, Henry VI (a succession challenged by the head of the house of York, Richard Plantagenet). Eltruda's father, Albert, is a Lancastrian, her lover, Edwin, a Yorkist. In her first published poem, then, Williams draws on a topos that will recur in much of her writing: private affections blasted by public strife. The significance of this topic is not just related to the revival of interest in all matters medieval, but stems from Williams' (and as we have seen, Smith's) interest in foregrounding the moral and emotional impact of historical conflict, and in imparting an understanding of historical conflict through the analogy of the private sphere. The topos of the family at war in *Edwin and Eltruda* has contemporary resonance in Britain's recent attempts to subdue the American revolution in the War of Independence, itself a 'civil conflict' as the American forces began the war as British subjects. This is a subject which Charlotte Smith took on in *The Old Manor House* and which Williams addresses directly in her poem *An American Tale* and in her novel *Julia*. The ballad's political contemporaneity is echoed in the 'modish' characterization as Edwin, Eltruda and Albert are characters drawn from the eighteenth-century culture of sensibility. The Lancastrian chief has martial prowess ('A bold avent'rous knight; /Renown'd for victory; his name/In glory's annals bright' (*EE*, ll.101–12)) but his sentimental credentials are soon established:

> Yet milder virtues he possest,
> And gentler passions felt;
> For in his calm and yielding breast
> The soft affections dwelt.
>
> (*EE*, ll.17–20)

The death of Albert's wife, Emma, forces him to look for solace in his infant daughter, Eltruda. This is a situation familiar to readers of sentimental fiction, including Williams' own novel *Julia*, where a benevolent man is left to bring up a daughter whose fine sensibility surpasses even her father's. The 'lovely, peerless maid' (*EE*, l.54) Eltruda is such a woman, and from her solitary abode she emerges to rescue stray lambs and falling linnets, and impart her 'lib'ral boon' (*EE*, l.117) to the 'lone widow' (*EE*, l.107) and the 'weeping mother' (*EE*, l.109). Edwin, a young man of 'lib'ral heart' (*EE*, l.69) but 'scanty...store' (*EE*, l.66) wins her heart and the two form a bond that transcends the 'sordid views, that now engage/The mercenary pair' (*EE*, ll.75–6). They are a self-conscious fantasy of better times, the 'youthful poet's soothing dream/Of golden ages past' (*EE*, ll.129–30). The pastoral idyll of the first 130 lines is ruptured, however, by:

> the fatal day
> For civil discord fam'd;

> When *York*, from *Lancaster*'s proud sway,
> The regal scepter claim'd.
>
> (*EE*, ll.137-40)

Williams focuses on the sorrows, not the glories of this civil war, and she paints her muse as lyrical and melancholic, rather than epic:

> The bard, who feels congenial fire,
> May sing of martial strife;
> And with heroic sounds, inspire
> The gen'rous scorn of life;
>
> But ill the theme would suit her reed,
> Who, wand'ring thro' the grove,
> Forgets the conq'ring hero's meed,
> And gives a tear to love.
>
> (*EE*, ll.201-8)

As a moral arbiter of the battle scene, she looks for the emotional impact not the national significance, so turns to the love story rather than to the detail of martial combat. When Edwin kills Albert in the course of battle, he is forced to confront Eltruda with the news of her father's death. She responds with a plan to recreate the pastoral retreat that was theirs before the war, albeit now marked by their loss:

> We'll shun the face of glaring day,
> Eternal silence keep;
> Thro' the dark wood together stray,
> And only live to weep.
>
> (*EE*, ll.349-52)

This fantasy is short-lived as the poem takes a Gothic turn, and Eltruda hears 'Some angel' (*EE*, l.355) and her 'father's spirit' (*EE*, l.358) demand their separation. Two stanzas later, Eltruda dies 'Of pale despair', and Edwin follows, overcome by grief:

> He feels within his shiv'ring veins,
> A mortal chillness rise;
> Her pallid corse he feebly strains –
> And on her bosom dies.
>
> (*EE*, ll.380-4)

A three-stanza coda restores the early harmony of the poem, however, as the poet envisions a happier afterlife: 'For heav'n in love, dissolves the ties/That chain the spirit here' (*EE*, ll.389–90). While these lines offer an unambiguous vision of release, the nature of the 'ties that chain the spirit' are more uncertain. They may well be the 'prejudicial' ties that divided the lovers: the ties to the Houses of York or Lancaster. They may also be the ties of romantic love, from which the afterlife provides release, an idea to which Williams returns in her 1790 novel, *Julia*.

AN AMERICAN TALE

Much of Williams' poetry in the 1780s explores the ties of nation, tribe and family and the more overtly oppressive ties of slavery or colonial bondage. Although the 'private ties' are invariably privileged over those of more public formations, often the ties of country are figured *as* familial ties. Such a poem is the shorter ballad that appeared in her 1786 collection, *An American Tale*.[7] It covers similar emotional ground to *Edwin and Eltruda*, though it is set three hundred years later during the American War of Independence. This war was inspired by Britain's protectionist economic policies that meant that her American subjects had to pay tariffs on their own manufactures. Many British commentators took a strongly counter-revolutionary, loyalist stand during the war.[8] The British historian William Robertson, on whose work Williams drew for her later poem *Peru*, struggled to accommodate the American War into his *History of America* (1777), implicitly because he shrank from the controversy of the subject, but overtly because 'inquiries and speculations concerning their [North Americans'] ancient forms of policy and laws, which exist no longer, cannot be interesting'.[9] The American David Ramsay's patriotic (to America) but not entirely celebratory *History of the American Revolution* did not appear until 1789. The most celebrated account available to Williams at the time of writing *An American Tale* would have been the French radical Raynal's updated 1780 edition of *Histoire philosophique des...deux Indes*, which justified the position of the American rebels in a new section on the American War. It is in the context, then, of a range of available positions on the American conflict that Williams offers up *An American Tale*.

The poem was dismissed by the *European* as 'an evident copy of Dr Goldsmith's *Hermit*' which trots out 'tears, and love, and sounds of woe, etc, etc, and those eternal topics of female poetry'. More generously put, it illustrates the 'female historian's' role as a 'moral arbiter' and, like *Edwin and Eltruda*, explicates 'civil' discord through familial breakdown. It has a more complex formal design than the earlier poem, however. It begins in *medias res*, with the voice of Amelia who is searching for her father, a British soldier who has been wounded in battle. She finds him held captive by American forces, but treated well by one who

> feels the captive Briton's woe:
> For his ennobled mind,
> Forgets the name of Britain's foe,
> In love of human kind.
>
> (*AT*, ll.35–8)

This benevolent, universalist youth is thought to be a friend of Amelia's American lover, Edward, who is understood to have been lost in battle. Amelia's father refers to the youth's 'erring sword' that he draws 'fierce against Britannia's band' (*AT*, ll.33–4) but the focus on his exceptional humanity, serenity, the absence of 'rude passion' (*AT*, ll.88) marks him out as 'more than' an enemy of the British and a friend of liberty. Amelia recalls how Edward had overcome the physical barrier between their nations to be with her:

> The western ocean roll'd in vain
> Its parting waves between,
> My Edward brav'd the dang'rous main,
> And bless'd our native scene.
>
> (*AT*, ll.71–4)

After listening to Amelia enumerate Edward's sentimental charms, the young man ('By darkness veil'd' (*AT*, l.45)) reveals himself as her lost lover. He explains how it was his father's injunction that had forced him to separate from Amelia. Edward's father is moved by the plight of his son to lift his prohibition:

> My father saw my constant pain,
> When thee I left behind,

> No longer will his power restrain,
> The ties my soul would bind.
>
> *(AT,* ll.111–14)

'The ties my soul would bind' are ties to Amelia: the ties of country are undone in the service of amorous romance. Edward is now free to choose where to attach his loyalty, and vows to Amelia to restore her father's liberty and create a new family:

> soon thy honor'd sire shall cease
> The captive's lot to bear,
> And we, my love, will soothe to peace
> His griefs, with filial care.
>
> *(AT,* ll.115–18)

The 'politics' of this new family arrangement are, if not republican, then democratic. The American Edward has overcome his own father's injunction and national enmity to tend to the needs of Amelia's father and promise a future to his daughter. On the one hand, then, national divisions are deemed irrelevant in the face of romantic attachment; on the other, the power relation between the nations is redrawn, with the strong but generous American son pledging a new kind of allegiance to the ageing Briton: no longer a subject but an independent son.

AN ODE ON THE PEACE

This optimistic version of a revised familial relationship between Britain and America is just one of a whole repertoire of new images for a 'post-imperial' Britain constructed by writers of the 1780s. Williams' *An Ode on the Peace* (1783) like *An American Tale* foregrounds the new beginning heralded by the loss of the North American colonies.[10] A celebration of the 1783 peace treaty between Britain and America, the *Ode* charts the rise and fall of a discordant spirit of the Atlantic ocean:

> Her crested serpents, discord throws
> O'er scenes which love with roses grac'd;
> The flow'ry chain his [the Atlantic's] hands compose,
> She wildly scatters o'er the waste:
>
> *(OP,* ll.17–20)

The 'awful sound' (*OP*, l.29) of the 'savage soul of war' (*OP*, l.25) thundering 'o'er the echoing ground' (*OP*, l.30) gives way to 'softer sounds of sorrow' (*OP*, l.33) and the poem takes a sentimental turn. It shifts its focus to the death of 'gentle André' (*OP*, l.57), the celebrated British Major, John André, who was convicted by the American congress as a spy and hanged in New York in October 1780. John André was known personally to and eulogized by Williams' acquaintance, Anna Seward, in her 1781 *Monody on Major André*. Seward's poem is a mourner's lament for the 'dear, lovely Youth! Whose gentle virtues stole/ Thro' Friendship's soft'ning medium on her soul!' (ll.35–6).[11] Williams pays tribute both to André and Seward's poem:

> While Seward sweeps her plaintive strings,
> While pensive round his sable shrine,
> A radiant zone she graceful flings,
> Where full emblaz'd his virtues shine;
>
> (*OP*, ll.65–8)

Seward's lament foregrounds André's doomed relationship with Honora, Seward's half-sister (which was a romance forestalled by parental intervention), the persistence of André's love for her, his attachment to his family, the brutal nature of his execution, and the paucity of his funeral rites. Williams' *Ode* condenses the details of the personal tragedy and, as is characteristic of the ode form, finds reconciliation from the discord of fury and grief:

> Cease, cease ye throbs of hopeless woe;
> He lives the future hours to bless,
> He lives, the purest joy to know,
> Parental transports fond excess;
>
> (*OP*, ll.89–92)

André's 'afterlife' is figured in the 'mild benignant Peace' (*OP*, l.103) between America and Britain. Williams calls on André's mourners ('Ye, who have mourn'd the parting hour/ Which love in darker horrors drew' (*OP*, ll.129–30)) to 'paint the youth's return by grief endear'd' (*OP*, l.136); that is, to envision a rebirth of André's spirit. In place of the 'sanguine wreath' (*OP*, l.145) on André's tomb will bloom the 'milder glories' hung around 'thy simple shrine/Fair Peace!' (*OP*, ll.147–8). André, the martyr of war-time rhetoric, is now a totem of reconciliation.

The cessation of hostilities is in itself not a particularly powerful source of national pride, especially when it signals British defeat. Williams, like many others, looked for more positive signs of British strength to restore its tarnished self-image. The remainder of the *Ode* is thus a tribute to British civilization carried forward by commerce (a powerful force for good for Williams) that at the end of war 'lifts her drooping head' (*OP*, 1.149). After the war, 'Albion' (significantly Williams uses Britain's ancient and mythical name, to evoke a national power and authority transcendent of history) is bestowed with its deserved bounty: 'The riches Nature gives each happier clime' (*OP*, 1.152). These riches are the fruits of new colonial enterprise as commerce braves the 'polar snow' of the North-West Passage and the 'torrid ray' of the Indian subcontinent to waft 'bright gems to Britain's temp'rate vale' (*OP*, 1.159). There is a glimpse in this poem of the hostilities yet to come, as while Albion is richly rewarded by commerce, 'ever hostile' Gallia (Albion's French equivalent) receives only her 'stern' glances. In 1780s Britain, however, the flourishing of commerce awakens the 'finer arts' (*OP*, 1.178), the 'historic Muse'(*OP*, 1.217), 'meek philosophy' (*OP*, 1.225) and 'Fair Science' (*OP*, 1.234).

This commonplace connection between the freedom of commerce and a flourishing culture – a connection that Williams was to reaffirm in her *Letters from France* – was contested by some of Williams' contemporaries, including Smith in *Beachy Head*. Anna Laetita Barbauld was emphatic in her critique. Even in the 1780s, Barbauld was equivocal in her assessment of the universal blessings of British commercial growth, particularly colonial expansion, and technological development. By the time she wrote *Eighteen Hundred and Eleven*, Barbauld was explicit in connecting British commercial interests with colonial exploitation, a connection that she prophesies will undermine a once flourishing British culture:

> fairest flowers expand but to decay;
> The worm is in thy core, thy glories pass away;
> Arts, arms and wealth destroy the fruits they bring;
> Commerce, like beauty, knows no second spring.[12]

PERU

Williams did address the avaricious potential of commerce when she shifted her attention from North to South America in her 1784 poem *Peru*.[13] Here, she anticipates the interest of poets like Barbauld and Percy Shelley who, in the early nineteenth century, expressed concern about the colonial exploitation of South America.[14] It may have been inspired by the 1780 uprising against the Spanish presence in Peru, a rule that that had lasted since the 1530s. The rebellion was led by Tupac Amaru II, the descendant of the last indigenous leader of the Incas. The six-canto epyllion, or miniature epic poem, tells the story of the fall of the Peruvian empire at the hands of the Spanish in the sixteenth century through a series of love stories. Like William Robertson, on whose account the poem is based, Williams characterizes the Spanish imperial enterprise as overly acquisitive, and driven by an unregulated desire for wealth at the expense of cultural development. The Spanish empire, like all early European imperialism, was built upon mercantilist principles, that is, the collection of precious metals and the state protection of trade. The attraction of Peru to Spanish colonizers was its gold, as they bypassed the trading process to secure wealth directly for the 'mother' nation. By the 1780s, mercantilist ideas of national economic strength had been supplanted by *laissez-faire* capitalism, freedom of trade and labour. Williams' portrait of a barbaric mercantilist nation in *Peru* throws into relief the allusions to Britain freely trading with its new colonial 'partners' in a number of her poems of the 1780s, a partnership that brings cultural capital to both sides, not just gold to one.

As Williams announces in the advertisement to the poem, *Peru* is not an attempt at 'a full, historical narration of the fall of the Peruvian empire' (53). Williams focuses on the stories of a few heroic individuals, primarily native Peruvians, who suffer at the hands of unscrupulous Spanish conquistadors and fanatical priests. While her primary sources are Robertson's *History* and Raynal's *Histoire*, *Peru* is also inflected by the so-called 'Black Legend', an image of the barbaric Spaniard most famously circulated in Bartolomé de Las Casas' *A Short Account of the Destruction of the Indies* (1552). Las Casas, a Spanish Dominican priest, drew attention to the inhumane exploitation of the indigenous populations of South America by the Spanish and after his death became an icon of anti-imperialist and human rights movements in Latin America. Las Casas gets a brief mention in Robertson's *History* as an advisor to the Spanish Emperor in 1542, when there was widespread concern that the ferocity of the Spanish forces threatened the extinction of the indigenous population. While Robertson praises Las Casas' advocacy for the Indians, he treats his account of the barbarity of the Spanish with scepticism, referring to the 'apparent marks of exaggerated description' in his discourse.[15] Williams raids the lexicon of the Black Legend without Robertson's inhibition. In Canto II, in a scene taken loosely from Robertson's history, a 'stern Pizarro' approaches the Peruvian monarch Zorai, and disguises his intent to plunder in 'themes of joy' (*Peru*, II, l.15) and with overtures of friendship. Zorai '[t]oo artless for distrust...springs/To meet his latent foe on friendship's wings' (*Peru*, II, ll.5–6). When the overawed monarch drops the Bible that was presented to him by the Spanish, 'frantic zeal each breast inspires' (*Peru*, II, l.25) and the colonizers attack.

This Manichean dualism shapes all six cantos of *Peru*, with the Spanish figured as 'the savage Condor, on terrific wings' (*Peru*, IV, l.175) preying on the Peruvian 'humming bird in beauty drest' who '[a]ttunes his soothing song to notes of love' (*Peru*, IV, l.169, l.171), a classic sentimental image of suffering. The only deserving Spaniard is Las Casas, in whose representation Williams dispenses with the historical source (Las Casas was in Madrid at the time of the massacre of the Incas) and figures him as a 'pitying angel' (*Peru*, III, l.97), a benevolent intercessor who tempers the worst excesses of Pizarro and the zealous priest, 'the fall'n angel' (*Peru*, III, l.121) Valverda. So in Canto III, Las Casas saves an aged Peruvian priest from torture and reappears in Canto V to intercede between the Spanish conqueror Alphonso and two lovers, Aciloe and Zamor. Alphonso has claimed Aciloe as his, but Las Casas obtains her freedom and leads them both to safety. The final Canto figures the death of Las Casas, his soul '[n]ow faint with virtue's toil' (*Peru*, VI, l.209). At his death he is tended by one of a number of the poem's allegorical figures: 'A bending angel consecrates his tears.../'Tis Sensibility!' (*Peru*, VI, l.211, l.217). Sensibility tends Las Casas' 'deserted grave' (*Peru*,

VI, l.229) and appeals to '[y]e gentle spirits whom my soul refines' (l.241), men and women of sensibility, to attend his shrine and learn from his example. As in *Edward and Eltruda* and *An American Tale*, so in *Peru*, virtue comes dressed in sentimental garb.

Like her historical sources, Williams brings a cosmopolitan perspective to her treatment of the victims of Spanish imperial zeal, casting her Peruvian protagonists in terms familiar to her British readers. Ataliba and Alzira, Manco-Capac and Cora, Zamor and Aciloe bear love, suffering and loss with the stoicism and magnanimity of Christian icons and conduct their amorous and family relationships in terms of European modernity. Cosmopolitanism may, of course, be problematically universalizing, erasing the subject's cultural difference and recasting it in the image of another, dominant culture. Politically dubious or not, this was a technique used by liberal and enlightened writers of the late eighteenth century in their arguments for what we think of as 'human rights', including arguments for the abolition of slavery.

A POEM ON THE BILL LATELY PASSED FOR REGULATING THE SLAVE TRADE

Anti-slavery debates were conducted in fiction and non-fiction, poetry and prose, and included Williams' own contribution, *A Poem on the Bill Lately Passed for Regulating the Slave Trade* (1788).[16] Novelists like Sarah Scott, Henry Mackenzie and Laurence Sterne, poets like Thomas Day, Hannah More and William Roscoe, pro- and anti-slavery propagandists like James Ramsay and Thomas Clarkson and the parliamentarian William Wilberforce all used sentimental discourse and its view of a common humanity to rouse the sympathies of a British audience for the cause of abolition. Williams' poem commemorates the 1788 Regulated Slave Trade Act, which reduced the number of slaves that could be carried on a slave ship on the transatlantic crossings that were regularly made in the 1780s. Britain had been involved in the 'triangular' trade of slaves from Africa (in exchange for British manufactured goods) to America (in return for sugar, molasses, cocoa and cotton) since the late seventeenth century, but by the 1780s what Williams called the 'barb'rous commerce' (*RST*, l.232) was at its peak. In the same decade, the Society for the Abolition of the Slave Trade was founded (in 1787) and launched a twenty-year campaign to bring the trafficking of African captives to an end. The pressure inside and outside parliament culminated in the 1807 bill to abolish British involvement in the slave trade (although it was still legal to have slaves). Williams' poem was part of this campaign and sets out to flatter and prick the conscience of the British government. Britain, 'first of EUROPE'S polish'd lands' (*RST*, l.37), is lauded for its initiative in passing the 1788 act:

> The noble, blest decree
> That soothes despair, is fram'd by thee!
> Thy powerful arm has interpos'd,
> And one dire scene for ever clos'd;
>
> (*RST*, ll.31–4)

Williams paints the 'dire scene' of slaves suffocating in the bowels of crowded slave ships in the first thirty lines of the poem, and uses the sentimental technique of figuring suffering individuals with whom her readers can identify, in particular the mother clutching an infant gasping for breath:

> woman, she, too weak to bear
> The galling chain, the tainted air, —
>
> . . . .
> With all the mother at her soul,
> With eyes where tears have ceas'd to roll,
> Shall catch the livid infant's breath,
> Then sink in agonizing death!
>
> (*RST*, ll.21–2; 27–30)

Williams does not turn this figure into a 'character', a named fictional individual. She is simply 'woman', a universal mother. This is an interesting shift for Williams, who, as we have seen, frequently draws readers into the story of a fictional character to allow them to participate in the process of moral arbitration in the poem. History is focalized through the emotional trials of (albeit sketchily developed) characters. Part of Williams' argument in this poem is the inadequacy of sympathy for or from an individual as the basis for human justice. In illustration, she figures the agonies of a slave trying to read the disposition of his new owner, to discern whether his eye reveals 'one blest glance of mercy' (*RST*, l.162) or whether 'savage habit' has steeled the 'vulgar mind' (*RST*, ll.172–3). Such vagaries of temper, she argues, are no foundation for human rights:

> Yet why on one poor chance must rest
> The int'rest of a kindred breast?
> Why yield to passion's wayward laws
> Humanity's devoted cause?
>
> (*RST*, ll.176–9)

The poem argues for universal benevolence, a dispassionate recognition of the slave's shared humanity and calls on Britain to lead the way in abolishing the trade in people and to build on the 'base of freedom' (the Regulation Act) it has laid:

> Lov'd BRITAIN! Whose protecting hand,
> Stretch'd o'er the globe, on AFRIC'S strand
> The honour'd base of freedom lays,
> Soon, soon the fabric raise!
>
> (*RST*, ll.282–5)

Williams characteristically portrays Britain as a civilizing force and makes a distinction between the benign colonial exploits of the 'gen'rous sailor' (*RST*, l.177) who bears the 'British flag o'er sultry seas/And spreads it on the Polar breeze' (*RST*, ll.179-80) and the 'barb'rous commerce' (*RST*, l.176) of the slave trader. Thus, '[t]hose whom the traffic of their race/Has robb'd of every human grace' (*RST*, ll.161–2) are contrasted with the British flag-bearer, '[h]e to whose guardian arm we owe/Each blessing that the happy know' (*RST*, ll.181–2).

There is a tension, then, between her view of commerce as a progressive force and the images of human commodities that dominate the poem: 'Man, dire merchandize! Is sold,/And barter'd life is paid for gold!' (*RST*, ll.204–5). This is symptomatic of broader attitudes to slave-trading that condemned it not just for inhumanity but because it undermines the spirit of *laissez-faire* capitalism and the idea of the freedom of the labour market that was so central to British economic thought after Smith's *The Wealth of Nations* (1776). Having lost its North American colonies, Britain's so-called 'first empire', the nation was well on the way to establishing another, larger empire centred on the Indian subcontinent and the Caribbean and there was enough potential to exploit the labour of those populations without the formal institution of slavery. Williams' opposition to slavery and her persistent faith in the civilizing force of 'free' commerce are thus connected. Her representation of benign British forces in *An American Tale*, of marauding Spanish imperialists in *Peru* and the abolitionist rhetoric of *A Poem on... Regulating the Slave Trade* are signs of both her enlightenment belief in universal human rights and of a patriotic yet cosmopolitan attachment to a Britain that was rebuilding its image as a liberal imperial force without the need for enforced or regulated labour. She carries these views with her to France in the 1790s, where, as I shall argue, her eight volumes of *Letters* consolidate her reputation, for good and ill, as a historian of private sentiment.

It is, perhaps, the unmediated representation of sentiment, unmediated that is by a self-conscious speaker, sceptical of its own powers of arbitration, like the speakers of Smith's sonnets, that distances us from Williams' poetry. In her only novel, *Julia*, sentiment is represented discursively, its different modes put into play, to produce a more fraught engagement with the performance of sensibility than we find in Williams' early poetry. As I shall argue, the more radical means of this novel do not necessarily produce revolutionary ends, as Williams finally opts for a fairly conservative model of female conduct to protect her protagonist, Julia, from the tyranny of her would-be lover's 'transparent' sentiments and passions.

7

Philosophical Passions: *Julia*

Helen Maria Williams' only novel, *Julia*, was published in 1790 and marks the transition in her writing career from poetry to prose.[1] It is in many ways a conventional novel of sensibility. The eponymous heroine is a woman of exceptionally fine feeling who acts on her benevolent disposition to relieve suffering wherever she finds it. Like Charlotte Smith's novels, *Julia* satirizes the mores and affectations of the aristocracy and fashionable society. The novel is sketched on a smaller canvas than Smith's, however, mirroring the limited movements of women like Julia Clifford and her cousin Charlotte. At the time of writing Williams was still living in London, and though her social world was broader than that of most women, she had not travelled abroad and, like most of her female peers, her experience of the world was mediated by literature. Like Julia, many heroines of later eighteenth-century fiction by women are avid readers, signifying both a nascent feminist acceptance of women's intellectual and imaginative capacities and the material constraints on other kinds of lived female experience.

The action of *Julia* largely takes place in and around London and the households of Mrs Melbourne, the Seymours, the Cliffords and the Chartres and in Mr Clifford's estate 'in the north' of England. There is some reported movement further afield: the Seymours and Mrs Melbourne go to Scotland and Bath, Mr Clifford, Captain Meynell and Chartres travel to the East Indies. Charlotte accompanies her father to France, where Julia is meant to meet them. Before Julia can make her journey, however, her father becomes ill and dies, and she is left to wait in England for the return of her uncle and cousin. Her 'experience' of the larger world, like that of most women in the late eighteenth century, remains vicarious. Frederick Seymour may 'lead her through half Europe' but only in her imagination (*Julia*, 1, 131–2).

Frederick Seymour and the devoted Mr F act for Julia as intermediaries between the public and private spheres. This is a boundary that Julia will struggle to police as the novel progresses, as Seymour, betrothed to her cousin Charlotte but in love with Julia, intrudes with increasing insistence on her internal world. While Williams' poetry of the 1780s made the public private by exploring the emotional impact of historical events, *Julia* has as its focus the border between the public and the private, not just in social terms but with respect to the life of the individual, the interior life and its exterior manifestation. As it is written on the cusp of the French Revolution, when the 'transparency' of the citizen, in Rousseau's terms, was to be scrutinized by the state, this was a prescient theme.[2]

PRIVATE/PUBLIC CORRESPONDENCE

Mr F's role as go-between is more innocuous in its execution than Seymour's, even if its intent, to get closer to Julia, is similar. On two occasions he brings the outside world into Julia's domestic containment by showing her some of his personal correspondence. The first is a packet of letters that happen to be about the American War; the second includes a lengthy poem about the notorious Parisian prison, the Bastille. Mr F's personal correspondence has an instructively public dimension. A packet of letters from Long Island, one dated August, 1776, provides the only reference in the novel to its historical setting and contains an account of the death of Mr F's brother while serving as a captain in the British army during the American War of Independence. A second letter in the packet is the history of Captain F's relationship with Sophia Herbert, daughter of a family from Virginia. The narrative of Sophia Herbert recalls the themes of a number of Williams' poems of the 1780s, *Edwin and Eltruda* and *Peru* and, more directly, *An American Tale*, where love transcends political division although the tragedy of war or conflict separates the lovers in this world. Sophia Herbert refuses to give up the love of the British Captain F for the love of her country; in the psychoanalytic terms used by Eleanor Ty, Sophia refuses to overlook 'the literal' (Captain F) 'in order to make the symbolic order (the British army that he represents) possible'.[3] Captain F dies on the battlefield and Sophia dies of a broken heart. The thematic relationship of this narrative to Julia's story is oblique. As I shall demonstrate, unlike the subjects of Williams' poetry and Sophia Herbert, Julia does not follow the dictates of her heart over duty and nor does she follow her suitor to his grave. She shares, however, Sophia's resistance to 'prejudice'. While Sophia refuses the prejudice of nation, Julia is indifferent to the prejudice of rank and social status.

The second piece of private correspondence Mr F reads to Julia and Charlotte is a poem 'written by a friend lately arrived from France' who had been locked in the Bastille and who envisions its fall. The love story and the vision both give the novel a historical specificity that is otherwise lacking from its account of Julia's round of social engagements. They also serve to raise the status of Julia's internal landscape: both argue for resistance to prejudice and celebrate the public value of the benevolence and refinement of sensibility that Julia brings to her everyday life.

READING INTERIORS

The limited geographical scope of Julia's life is matched by its circumscribed frame of reference. Williams writes:

> Fashionable conversation is not very extensive: it goes on rapidly for a while, in a certain routine of topics, and reminds us of our street-musicians, who, by turning a screw, produce a set of tunes on the hand-organ; but when they have gone through a limited number, the instrument will do no more, the same sounds may be repeated to a new set of auditors. (*Julia*, 1, 23)

The lack of 'depth' and variety in social discourse evoked in this image is significant in a novel which, like many other pieces of sentimental writing, is interested in exploring the interiority and emotional complexity of its characters and of finding ways to represent that internal life stylistically. The epistolary form was important in the development of this technique, but Williams dispenses with it for a third-person narration which figures interiority through conversation, gesture and social behaviour. The technical challenge involved in this technique mirrors the novel's thematic interest in the difficulty of reading the internal life of other people.

One of the sources of narrative tension in the novel is the test to Julia's power of will and her strength of moral purpose that is effected by her acute ability to 'read' other people, in particular Frederick Seymour. Seymour is betrothed to, and eventually marries, Charlotte but falls irrevocably in love with Julia. Julia reciprocates his feelings but denies them for the sake of her duty to, and love for, her cousin. In its evocation of repressed desire, *Julia* is reminiscent of Rousseau's *La Nouvelle Héloïse*, and its depiction of a woman torn between love for a man and duty to a woman recalls Frances Sheridan's *Memoirs of Miss Sidney Bidulph*, itself modelled on Richardson's tale of suffering female sensibility, *Clarissa*. Unlike its predecessors, however, Williams' novel does not end with the death or social descent of its heroine. It is Frederick Seymour who dies, 'the victim of that fatal passion, which he at first unhappily indulged, and which he was at length unable to subdue' (*Julia*, 2, 278). The two women live on harmoniously and devote themselves to the care of Charlotte and Seymour's son.[4]

Though *The Monthly Review* thought the conclusion 'melancholy' (and hastily achieved) recent readers have read the reconciliation of the two women and the demise of Frederick Seymour as a celebration of the triumph of female sensibility over patriarchal expectation, as Julia and Charlotte establish, in Eleanor Ty's words, a 'life dependent upon connection rather than competition'.[5] It is certainly friendship that triumphs over romantic attachment or marriage, as the Clifford women take in Mrs Meynell, the wronged poor relation of the Seymours, whose brutal husband has been consigned to the East Indies. They are frequently visited by another of Julia's erstwhile suitors, Mr F, who has given up the pursuit of love in favour of retaining her friendship. Julia, we are told 'refused many honourable offers of marriage' and 'found consolation in the duties of religion, the exercise of benevolence, and the society of persons of understanding and merit' (*Julia*, 2, 282). I agree with Ty that Williams, in having her heroine reject marriage and establish herself in a female-run community (it also includes Charlotte's son) 'reveals her ambivalent feelings about the androcentric bias of her society'.[6] The chaste denouement, however, also reveals her anxiety about the effects of powerful emotion on men and women. In 1790, such effects were understood to impact on the public as well as the private sphere and while *Julia* foregrounds interpersonal struggles with intense feelings it uses language and ideas which would come to be associated with early revolutionary philosophy, and particularly with Rousseau: the ideals of social transparency, universal benevolence and the rejection of national prejudice. Significantly, strong or excessive feeling, referred to as 'passion', is characterized in the novel, in political terms, as an absolutist force:

> the region of passion is a land of despotism, where reason exercises but a mock jurisdiction; and is continually forced to submit to an arbitrary tyrant, who, rejecting her fixed and temperate laws, is guided only by the dangerous impulse of his own violent and uncontroulable [sic] wishes. (*Julia*, 2, 163–4)

This characterization of passion as a despotic land and 'an arbitrary tyrant' is typical of the way in which, in sentimental discourse of the late eighteenth century, strong or extreme emotion was identified as a force external to the will of the individual who 'suffered' under it.[7] In 1790, the use of a political analogy evokes the terms of early revolutionary debates; Williams casts 'reason' as the temperate force of democratic will pitted against the *ancien régime* of violent emotion.[8] It is not Frederick Seymour, but his 'passion' for Julia that is the despotic force, and he and Julia are both victimized by the intensity of the emotion and its moral implication (a theme also explored by Smith in *Desmond*). While 'passion' is thus demonized, Williams simultaneously offers portraits of the social and moral benefits of a more benign sentimentality in the figures of Julia and the Clifford family, whose feelings are figured as an extension of their internal will.

AFFECTED SENSIBILITY

The relationship between will and feeling is one of the sources of social satire in the novel, as characters 'affect' the fashionable signs of sensibility. The characters are loosely divided between those who circulate in, or aspire to membership of the *ton*, and those who are indifferent to its affectations. One of the most aspirational characters is Miss Melbourne, later Mrs Charles Seymour, for whom sentiment is a sign of refinement; if it is not inherited from nature, she believes, it can be acquired. Refined people, she observes, are 'often extremely miserable; she, therefore, deemed discontent the test of feeling, and, with scarcely a wish ungratified, she thought that to be happy, with what would make any vulgar mind happy, would be only proving that she was dull' (*Julia*, 1, 18). Sensibility is here performative, a social quality, affected at will to effect social esteem. Mrs Melbourne, Mrs Chartres and their associates and the eldest and youngest Seymour brothers also exemplify such orchestrated sensibilities. The women's affectations achieve largely comic effects, epitomized by Mrs Chartres' bathetic recommendation of the new novel, *The Pangs of Sensibility*: 'It will only cost you six shillings, and it's so excessively pretty; but the end's very dismal' (*Julia*, 2, 180). Two of the three Seymour brothers affect sensibility to more sinister ends, however. The youngest, Charles Seymour, uses the language of sensibility in the service of courting a potentially wealthy wife, but is impervious to the designs of sentimental ritual:

> he was one of those prudent young men, who are too well trained in the school of the world, to be the dupes of any tender sensibility...: the darts poured from bright eyes fell blunted on his heart, unless the fair object had the more solid recommendation of fortune. (*Julia*, 1, 28)

The eldest brother, Mr Seymour, is an even more calculating and duplicitous figure. His performance as a man of sensibility takes in even the 'penetrative' Julia, until his libertine designs are revealed to her in the history of Mrs Meynell, the would-be victim of his seduction. His is an expert charade of sensibility:

> No man could talk with more energy of the virtues of generosity and disinterestedness than Mr Seymour; and this not with an appearance of ostentation, but as if friendship and universal good-will were the genuine feelings of his soul. Yet, while he thus descanted on benevolence, he concealed a mind, the sole view of which was self interest; and sometimes reminded those who knew his real

character, of a swan gracefully expanding his plumes of purest whiteness to the winds, and carefully hiding his black feet beneath another element. (*Julia*,1, 31–2)

The image of dissonance between surface and depth is revisited later in the narrative, and perhaps unexpectedly, in relation to Julia Clifford. While the eldest and youngest Seymour brothers attempt to deceive others, Julia tries to deceive herself that the 'uneasiness' she feels after a typically fraught encounter with the middle sibling, Frederick Seymour, is no other:

> than what arose from the agitation with which she perceived that Seymour's mind was struggling; but perhaps there was something of self-deception in this young lady's reflections; as to a passenger, in a boat that glides rapidly down a stream, the current only appears to move, and the boat seems perfectly still, while in reality the waves bear it impetuously along. (*Julia*, 1, 74)

This refusal to acknowledge her true feelings, her love for Frederick, for the greater good, marks Julia out as a more complex character than the rest of the Clifford family, who are identified as 'true' characters of sensibility by the congruence between surface and depth, and between performance and feeling. From the grandfather's kindness to his tenants, to Captain and Mr Clifford's benign paternalism and to Charlotte's 'sweetness of temper', the family share a natural benevolence, signified in each by their unconsciousness of its presence or its worth. Julia, in particular, delights in relieving distress, and when she eventually comes into money, rejoices 'in the possession of fortune, because she could now indulge the feelings of compassion' (*Julia*, 1, 53). Perhaps what differentiates Julia from Charlotte, her father and her uncle, is her greater insight. Charles Seymour is also described as having 'great penetration into character' but while he uses his powers of discernment for the purposes of self-aggrandizement (*Julia*,1, 31) Julia uses her sharp perception, her 'quick' sensibility, to sympathize with and relieve the distress of others (*Julia*, 1, 2). In the face of Frederick Seymour's distress, however, Julia is left unable to act. She recognizes the signs of his growing passion ('A thousand little circumstances in his behaviour had betrayed to her penetration the emotions of his heart' (*Julia*, 1, 71)) but she cannot or will not respond. Instead, 'she determined to lock the fatal secret within her own breast' (*Julia*, 1, 69) and maintains a stoic silence on the subject.

IMPERIOUS PASSION

The shared secret between Julia and Frederick gives a 'Gothic' quality to the rest of the novel. Julia fears his passion will be discovered and revealed to Charlotte and Mr Clifford (which it is, by another 'penetrative' but less scrupulous character, Miss Tomkins). Fredrick becomes ever more deranged in his attempts to make Julia respond to her knowledge of his passion as he watches her, follows her, and fetishizes her belongings, including a dropped glove that he takes without her knowledge: 'Seymour, when he reached his own apartment, locked the door, pulled the precious prize from his bosom, pressed it to his heart and lips ten thousand times, and was guilty of the most passionate extravagancies.' (*Julia*, 1, 109) Although we are left to imagine the nature of these 'most passionate extravagancies' they are another example of Frederick's loss of emotional control. While he shares Julia's candour and sensitivity (he 'disdained to tread in the serpentine paths of duplicity and cunning' (*Julia*, 1, 51)) he does not have her power of will:

> His mind resembled a fine-toned instrument, whose extensive compass was capable of producing the most sublime and elevating sounds; but a fatal pressure relaxed the strings, and sunk its powerful harmony.
>
> The ardent, enthusiastic spirit of this young man was susceptible of the strongest and most lasting impressions. How carefully, therefore, should he have guarded against the weak indulgence of that imperious passion, which, on such a temper, produces the most fatal effects, and subdues all energy of soul! (*Julia*, 2, 204)

The syntax of the last sentence here suggests that Fredrick initially has a choice not to indulge 'that imperious passion', but when he fails to resist, or to use his internal will, he is overcome. Julia's will to resist comes firstly from her duty to Charlotte and her faith in 'universal benevolence', which for her seems to preclude an exclusive attachment, especially a romantic attachment. Thus, when Frederick looks with envy on the domestic happiness of a peasant family ('What felicity to live for one beloved object... to meet with everlasting support and sympathy, with the charm of unbounded confidence'), Julia silences him with 'No more, Sir... I have no pleasure in being led into the regions of romance' (*Julia*, 1, 82). Fredrick's vision of devotion to one object is, for Julia, fanciful, and implicitly asocial. It eventually proves fatal for Frederick. His demise is prefigured in a conversation between him and Julia on the merits of the eighteenth century's most notorious work of sentimental fiction, *The Sorrows of Young Werther*, which charts the passion and the eventual suicide of its protagonist, and which was one source of inspiration for Smith's *Elegiac Sonnets*. '[E]very one must acknowledge that it is well written' concedes Julia, 'but few will justify its principles'. Frederick declares himself one of those few, and goes on to defend the novel as an empathic response to those too far gone in their passions to respond to the voice of reason:

> 'Why does Werter interest us? Because he is not a phoenix of romance, but has the feelings and infirmities of man. He is subject to the power of passion – let those who never felt its influence, condemn him; those who *have* felt its influence, too well know that it is absolute, that it is unconquerable.' (*Julia*, 2, 260)

Julia, who prefers the calming influence of Thomson's *Seasons* to the tumults of Goethe's fiction, refuses to believe in the 'absolute' force of passion. This is emphasized in the first poem attributed to Julia in the novel, 'An Address to Poetry', where the speaker implores 'Poesy', 'all my breast control' (*Julia*, 1, 9, l.13) and dismisses

> The selfish passion
> Whose force the social ties unbind,
> And chill the love of human kind,
> And make fond Nature's best emotions vain;
>
> (*Julia*, 1, 9, ll.5–8)

Poesy is a socially binding and calming spirit, and its finest insights come

> In those still moments when the breast
> Expanded, leaves its cares behind,
> Glows by some higher thought possest,
> And feels the energies of mind;
> Then, awful MILTON, raise the veil

> That hides from human eye the heav'nly throng!
> Immortal sons of light! I hear your song,
> I hear your high-tun'd harps creation hail!
>
> (*Julia*, 1, 9, ll.73-80)

In a state of calm, the speaker is open to poetic 'revelation', an insight into the quasi-divine force of creativity.[9] The religious register here is used again in another context with a more political subtext, when Julia, prompted by Mr Seymour's attempts to ensnare Mrs Meynell, envisions a moment when the 'veil' of oppression shall be rent and hidden suffering shall be revealed:

> while Julia's heart throbbed with indignation at the oppressor, and melted with compassion for the oppressed, she fancied she saw the arm of indignant Heaven tearing the veil by which iniquity was concealed, and making manifest the sufferings of innocence. (*Julia*, 2, 195)

TRANSPARENCY

The utopian language here is part of a broader discourse in the novel of divine 'revelation' and social 'transparency', the latter an ideal derived from the *philosophes*, in particular Rousseau, who associates the progress of civilization with a tendency to less candid social communication and more 'performative' exchanges. 'Transparency', an ideal we have seen put to the test in Smith's *Desmond*, was to become a watchword in revolutionary France under Robespierre, and extended to his ideals of public, political representation (including the physical space of the public assembly in which all representatives were open to the scrutiny of others). It later became another form of political tyranny, as the desire for openness motivated the interrogation of those who seemed to resist the authority of the new state.

Williams in some ways anticipates the 'tyrannical' potential of the ideal of transparency as Frederick Seymour's increasingly frantic demands for Julia's recognition of his inner feelings become a means to oppress his object of desire. An episode at a society ball illustrates the way in which Frederick's persistence compromises Julia's own openness and becomes semantically linked to a form of imprisonment for both Julia and Frederick. After a 'frenzied' encounter between the two earlier in the day, both attend the ball where Frederick first dances with and then sits by Julia and tries to engage her in conversation. However, 'her manner towards him was cold and distant', a stark contrast to her normal demeanour:

> Julia's usual manners had the most engaging frankness: her heart seemed to hover on her lips, and every emotion of her soul was clearly seen in her expressive countenance. Frederick Seymour had observed that she conversed with Mr F— with the utmost sweetness and vivacity; (*Julia*, 1, 96)

The 'degree of agony' to which her coolness brings Frederick provokes him to plead with Julia not only to drop her indifferent façade but to enter into his interior world: 'If you could look into my mind, if you could know what passes within this bosom, you would perhaps think that I am punished enough' (*Julia*, 1, 96–7). Julia can only respond to this appeal to her powers of penetration by agreeing to forget his misdemeanours and walking away. To remain true to Charlotte, Julia needs to be less, not more, aware of Frederick's internal agonies and increasingly opaque with respect to her own feelings.

Frederick's allusion to his self-imposed punishment is given a broader resonance in this scene by the setting of the ball: it takes place in one half of 'the town-house' (town-hall) whilst the other half houses the assizes, and prisoners awaiting trial. The ballroom becomes a kind of prison for both Frederick and Julia, anticipated in the earlier image of Julia in 'shackles' having committed herself to dance with Mr Chartres (*Julia*, 1, 76).

Transparency and the forms of social propriety are mutually tyrannical for Julia who is morally obliged to ignore her insight into Frederick's agonies while he insists on declaring them to her at every opportunity. Although the 'tyranny' is of a different order, there are thematic connections between Mr Seymour's entrapment of Mrs Meynell and Frederick's pursuit of Julia, reinforcing Eleanor Ty's view of the novel as a rejection of broad patriarchal values. The thematics of imprisonment and entrapment become more specific, however, when Mr F reads to Julia and Charlotte the poem that he has received from a friend recently released from the Bastille, which imagines the prison's fall. Given that the novel is set in 1776 (which is revealed in another piece of Mr F's personal correspondence), 'The Bastille' is presented as a prophecy of a moment in history that is yet to be written (though at the time of writing the prison had already fallen). In the vision, a personified Freedom calls on 'millions with according mind' to 'claim the rights of human kind' (*Julia*, 2, 270, ll.71–2) and destroy the Bastille. The speaker summons 'Philosophy' to oversee Freedom's work:

> Tis thine each truth to scan,
> Guardian of bliss, and friend of man!
> 'Tis thine all human wrongs to heal,
> 'Tis thine to love all nature's weal;
> To give each gen'rous purpose birth,
> And renovate the gladden'd earth.
>
> (*Julia*, 2, 271, ll.91–6)

'Philosophy', here, is the monitor of truth, the mediator in conflict and parent of generosity. It is a term that has arisen elsewhere in the novel in related contexts. When the gauche but well-meaning 'social visionary' Mr Chartres tells Julia of the report of Frederick Seymour's feelings for her, he attributes her with having 'philosophy enough to despise' the rumours (*Julia*, 2, 230). Here he foregrounds the sense of 'philosophy' as serenity and calm, but his use of the term is not unrelated to his own 'projected improvements in philosophy', meaning 'natural philosophy', or science, the systematic pursuit of knowledge (*Julia*, 2, 228). While Chartres' philosophical ambitions are a source of comedy, given his inability to understand the science of social manners or human behaviour, Julia's philosophical disposition, her refusal to succumb to the vagaries of passion, allies her – more than semantically – to the force of liberty that is evoked in the visionary poem.

PHILOSOPHICAL CONDUCT

The vision comes just prior to a crucial moment in Julia and Charlotte's relationship and again connects the private to the public passions. Charlotte gives birth to a son and shortly afterwards contracts a fever, from which she recovers. It is Frederick Seymour who succumbs to illness, or rather, who is finally overwhelmed by passion: 'Alas! the distempered heart, when it has suffered the disorders of passion to gain strength, can find no balsam in nature to heal their malignancy; no remedy but death.' (*Julia*, 2, 279) Julia's response to the sight of Frederick's corpse is typically stoical: 'she shuddered, she groaned deeply, but she uttered not a word' (*Julia*, 2, 280).

As I have suggested, Julia's 'philosophical' composure connects her to the 'revolutionary' forces of individual will and liberty from oppression in the novel. However, a quotation from Dr Gregory's *Legacy to his Daughters*, one of the most celebrated conduct books of the late eighteenth century, that Williams uses to contextualize Julia's 'wretched' but phlegmatic disposition, might signal that Julia conforms to a more conservative model of female propriety:

> Women have even greater reason than men to fortify their hearts against those strong affections, which, when not regulated by discretion, plunge in aggravated misery that sex, who, to use the words of an elegant and amiable writer, [Gregory] 'cannot plunge into business, or dissipate themselves in pleasure and riot, as men too often do, when under the pressure of misfortunes; but must bear their sorrows in silence, unknown and unpitied; must put on a face of serenity and chearfulness, when their hearts are torn with anguish, or sinking in despair.' (*Julia*, 2, 279)

While Gregory's imperatives ('must') are meant to signal his sympathy for the predicament of the 'wretched' woman, they are also consistent with his broader advice to his 'daughters' not to display their sentiments. The reference to Gregory might explain why Mary Wollstonecraft took issue with Williams' portrait of female stoicism in her review of *Julia* in the *Analytical Review*. In *A Vindication of the Rights of Woman* of 1792, Wollstonecraft rails against Gregory's advice to women to conceal their 'true selves': 'He actually recommends dissimulation, and advises an innocent girl to give the lie to her feelings, and not dance with spirit, when gaiety of heart would make her feet eloquent without making her gestures immodest.'[10] That Julia resists the tyranny of passion and eschews romantic attachment looks less 'radical' when viewed in this light, and more like a concession to a tradition of conduct guides which recommend the repression of female sexual desire and the concealment of extravagant feelings.

In Williams' next work, it would be her critics' response to her own extravagant feelings (sexual and political) that would see the turning point in her literary reputation. Four months after *Julia* went to press, in March 1790, Williams travelled to France at the invitation of family friends, the du Fossés. She was in Paris for the Fête de la Fédération and stayed literally and metaphorically close to the centre of the French revolution thereafter. During the 1790s, Williams' attachment to the 'philosophical life' is put to the test, a trial that she charts in the eight-volume *Letters from France*.

8

Revolution and Romance: *Letters from France*

Williams' most celebrated work, her eight-volume *Letters From France*, brings together her belief in the liberating force of commerce that was hinted at in her poetry of the previous decade, and in the possibility of 'transparent' social communication that she explored, if finally rejected, in *Julia*.[1] Written between 1790 and 1796, the letters see these beliefs put to the test, as the 'liberal' days of the early revolution, when Williams freely mingles with the crowds celebrating the Fête de la Fédération, turn into the repressive regime of the French Jacobins.

In 1789, when the French National Assembly began to overturn the power of the *ancien régime* by adopting the Declaration of the Rights of Man and accepting the principles of religious freedom and less aristocratic authority, Helen Maria Williams was living at the heart of London's dissenting community. This group was alive to the changes in France, changes that they sought for their own country. It was a private invitation from her friends, the du Fossés, that took Williams, along with her mother and sister, to France in July 1790, and this private visit was to be the germ of her public narrative of the French revolution.

The first volume, which is the main focus of my discussion here, was favourably received, though most reviews focused on the style of the *Letters* over the content, and nearly all made special pleading for Williams' youth and femininity in terms that diminish any political significance the texts could have. *The Analytical Review* notes that she demonstrates 'the talent of chatting on paper' that women have long possessed.[2] The style of the letters is 'unaffected' and with 'an air of sincerity', 'sprightly and entertaining'.³ Williams is characterized as a 'lively and agreeable companion', and an 'amiable letter-writer', comments that seem to build on her image as a London socialite. Even the most positive reviews, however, dismiss her enthusiasm for the revolution as 'the childish admiration of a confined mind' rather than 'the prudent and philosophical opinion of a writer, who certainly aims at instructing, as well as entertaining'.⁴ For the *General Magazine*, the problem with the *Letters* lies in Williams' attempt to 'charm the multitude', that is, to be popular rather than to aim for a more exclusive 'philosophical' readership.⁵ The most damning commentary came from the reviewer of the conservative *Gentleman's Magazine*, who dismissed Williams as just one of many 'English lad[ies]...fond of, or intoxicated with liberty' and doubted the veracity of the incidents she relates, so taken is she with the 'levity, fickleness, and fantasticalness of the French'.⁶

The tenor of these reviews suggests that Williams' style, in Volume 1 in particular, was an attempt to disarm her critics by dressing political opinion in an acceptably feminine garb. Her 'love of the French revolution', she maintains, is 'entirely an affair of the heart' and she has 'not been so absurd as to consult my head upon matters of which it is so incapable of judging' (*LFF*, 1, 91). To assert that her political creed is 'an affair of the heart' not of the head does seem to be a concession to those who expect women to respond to the world irrationally. So too does her claim not to have had an interest in politics before visiting Paris:

> Did you expect that I should ever dip my pen in politics, who used to take so small an interest in public affairs, that I recollect a gentleman of my acquaintance surprized me not a little, by informing me of the war between the Turks and the Russians, at a time when all the people of Europe, except myself, had been two years in possession of this intelligence? (*LFF*, 1, 109)

Given that Williams wrote a number of overtly political poems in the 1780s, such statements do seem to be designed to appease her detractors and to diminish the political impact of her views. However, another explanation for this profession of political naivety might be found in trying to understand the relationship between the language of feeling and politics in her writing.

Williams claims to 'feel' rather than 'judge' the revolution, not simply to appear more feminine and therefore less threatening to her readership, but to foreground the significance of emotion and sensation in the public world, as she had in her poetry of the 1780s and in her novel *Julia*. The revolution, she writes, was brought about by a shift in the feelings of the French public and is sustained by the establishment of a new culture that represents those feelings. The epistolary voice that Williams adopts in the *Letters* is not just of a woman of modest political understanding, but of a sentimental participant in an event that makes politicians of those who share the new sensibility of the French Republic.

THE THEATRE OF REVOLUTION

The iconic opening of Volume 1 illustrates the ways in which we are meant to understand the significance of sentiment in the revolution and the persona that Williams constructs for her letter writer. She arrives in France just in time for the first anniversary celebration of the fall of the Bastille. The Fête de la Fédération includes a dramatic reconstruction of the day before the Bastille was taken: 'a recitative which affected the audience in a very powerful manner, by recalling the images of that consternation and horror which prevailed in Paris on the 13th of July, 1789' (*LFF*, 1, 63–4). *The Taking of the Bastille*, as the drama was called, was preceded by an overture performed by a vast orchestra and followed by the 'sound of a loud and heavy bell', in imitation of the bells that rang through Paris the day before the Bastille was taken. At the sound of the bell and the accompanying cacophony from the orchestra, Williams writes, 'the audience appeared to breathe with difficulty; every heart seemed frozen with terror' (*LFF*, 1, 64). The theatrical and musical performance allows those, like Williams, who were not in Paris the year before, to share in the sensation of the original event and provides a choreographed version of history. In a way that the original event cannot, it addresses itself 'at once to the imagination, the understanding, and the heart!' (*LFF*, 1, 65).

If this theatricality seems at odds with the values of spontaneity and unselfconsciousness that a sentimentalist like

Williams might be expected to espouse – and which was so praised by her critics – we need to recognize that Williams' emphasis is on the emotion experienced by the audience rather than the quality of the performance.[7] Drawing on Burke's *Enquiry*, where he identified descriptions of the effects of beauty on the spectator as more powerful than descriptions of beauty, Williams notes how the sublimity of the scene 'depended much less on its external magnificence than on the effect it produced on the minds of the spectators. 'The people, sure, the people were the sight!' (*LFF*, 1, 64).[8] The theatricals are choreographed, but the response of the audience is spontaneous and therefore more awe-inspiring. She brings this aesthetic to her judgement of theatre itself. If Paris outstrips London on most things for Williams, its tragedians have not yet perfected the art of sentimental performance as well as the celebrated British actress Mrs Siddons:

> Before we can admire Madame Vestris, the first tragic actress of Paris, we must have lost the impression (a thing impossible) of Mrs Siddons's performance; who, instead of 'tearing a passion to rags,' like Madame Vestris, only tears the hearts of the audience with sympathy. (*LFF*, 1,102)

French comedy fares better than tragedy in Williams' eyes, largely because of the opportunities for audience participation:

> Most of the pieces we have seen at the French theatres have been little comedies relative to the circumstances of the times,... These little pieces might perhaps read coldly enough in your study, but have a most charming effect with an accompaniment of applause from some hundreds of the national guards, the real actors in the scenes represented. (*LFF*, 1, 102)

In political terms, the shift of emphasis from the pomp of the performance to the emotional response of the spectators – here, emotionally 'disarmed' French national guards – is an extension of Williams' and the early revolutionaries' democratic spirit. This democratic impulse can be found in other episodes from Volume 1, in which Williams, taking in the sights of Paris, seems drawn to the popular, and indeed commercial, rather than the high cultural quarters of the capital.[9] A visit to the Palais Royal, for instance, elicits only a brief commentary on the paintings in the gallery before she is side-tracked into an account of the superiority of the poetic over the visual arts in 'calling forth my sensibility' (*LFF*, 1, 97). The square outside, however, has Williams in raptures over the sociability of the scene and she cannot resist detailing the wares of the traders:

> You walk under piazzas round this square, which is surrounded with coffee-houses, and shops displaying a variety of ribbons, trinkets, and caricature prints, which are now as common at Paris as at London. The walks under the piazzas are crouded [sic] with people: and in the upper part of the square, tents are placed, where coffee, lemonade, ices, etc are sold. Nothing is heard but the voice of mirth; nothing is seen but chearful faces (*LFF*, 1, 96)

FRENCH EFFEMINACY

The sociability is engendered in part by the 'marketplace' that brings people together as consumers, not just spectators (a vivacity that resonates in Smith's portrait of Betty, who buys – or is bought – out of servitude in *The Old Manor House*). Williams is here celebrating an aspect of the French national character that had long been caricatured by Francophobic British commentators, who characterized the French as frivolous and materialistic in contrast to the sober and frugal British. These oppositions were played out in the revolution debate, with even pro-revolutionaries Thomas Paine and Mary Wollstonecraft wheeling out the old stereotypes. As Jacqueline Leblanc has argued, the stereotypes were also gendered, so that the French were 'effeminate' and the British 'masculine', or in Edmund Burke's term, 'manly' (Leblanc, 'Politics and Commercial Sensibility...', 27). Williams, then, buys into the same images but reverses their value. French effeminacy underpins the sociability and receptiveness to change of its national character, whilst British, or more particularly English, masculinity is consistent with the rigidity and formality of Williams' home nation. The experience of Williams and her sister at the National Assembly illustrates the distinction:

> my sister and I were admitted without tickets, by the gentleman who had command of the guard, and placed in the best seats, before he suffered the doors to be open to other people. We had no personal acquaintance with this gentleman, or any claim to his politeness,

except that of being foreigners and women; but these are, of all claims, the most powerful to the urbanity of French manners. (*LFF*, 1, 80–1)

Had a French woman been waiting for admission to Westminster Hall without a ticket, she jokes, 'she might stand there as long as Mr Hastings's trial has lasted, without being permitted to pass the barrier' (*LFF*, 1, 81), a reference both to the lengthy trial of Warren Hastings and the xenophobia and bigotry in the British character.[10]

If Williams can forgo her Englishness to become a French citizen, it is because French citizens are now 'citizens of the world'. But, as illustrated in the episode at the National Assembly, Williams feels most entitled to participate in French life on grounds of her gender. The leaders of the French revolution, she claims, 'are men well acquainted with the human heart' who rely not only on reason but 'have studied to interest in their cause the most powerful passions of human nature' (*LFF*, 1, 90). That is, they are men of sensibility who value beauty over sublimity, evidenced in the processions of young women who symbolize the liberty of the nation:

> five hundred young ladies walked dressed in white, and decorated with cockades of the national ribbon, leading by silken cords a number of prisoners newly released from captivity;...
>
> Thus have the leaders of the revolution engaged beauty as one of their auxiliaries, justly concluding, that, to the gallantry and sensibility of Frenchmen, no argument would be found more efficacious than that of a pretty face. (*LFF*, 1, 90)

Williams is quick to point out, however, that femininity is not *simply* an auxiliary of the revolutionary cause. The contribution of women to the establishment of the new order is a running theme of the *Letters*, and Volume 1 pays tribute to the aristocratic ladies, who have gladly sacrificed titles and personal wealth 'for the common cause':

> It was the ladies who gave the example of *le don patriotique*, by offering their jewels at the shrine of liberty; and, if the women of ancient Rome have gained the applause of distant ages for such actions, the women of France will also claim the admiration of posterity. (*LFF*, 1, 78–9)

Of particular note is Madame Sillery, or Madame Brulart as she became known after a decree of the National Assembly abolished aristocratic titles. Brulart was a writer on education and, at the time that Williams met her, tutor to the children of the King's cousin, the duc D'Orléans. Other pro-revolutionary commentators, including Mary Wollstonecraft, focused on the dissipated lifestyle of Orléans, as part of a justification for the abolition of the monarchy, but Williams highlights his libertarianism, implied in his choice of tutor for his children.[11] It was under Brulart's tutelage that the eldest prince learned 'to renounce the splendour of his aristocratic titles for the general good' (*LFF*, 1, 78), although he eventually became king in 1830. The 'democratic Prince' is the model for Williams of the new French royalty, limited in its authority, but with a constitutional role to play. Williams idealizes such a new relationship between monarch and people in the king's taking of the national oath:

> In an instant every sword was drawn, and every arm lifted up. A respectful silence was succeeded by the cries, the shouts, the acclamations of the multitude: they wept, they embraced each other, and then dispersed.
>
> You will not suspect that I was an indifferent witness of such a scene. (*LFF*, 1, 68–9)

Again, the reception of the event by the people, including Williams, is the most significant aspect of it, signalling a more than national unity:

> this was not a time in which the distinctions of country were remembered. It was the triumph of human kind; it was man asserting the noblest feelings of his nature; and it required but the common feelings of humanity to become in that moment a citizen of the world. (*LFF*, 1, 69)

ROMANCE EXPECTATIONS

In Williams' travels through and around Paris in 1790, there are still signs of the régime that was left behind only the year before. Williams is unable to enjoy the splendour of Versailles, 'that magnificent abode of a despot', because she conjures an image of the Bastille in the background. There are also glimpses of the Paris to come. La Lanterne, the place of execution during the early days of the revolution, chills Williams' blood: 'for the first time, I lamented the revolution; and forgetting the imprudence, or the guilt, of those unfortunate men, could only reflect with horror on the dreadful expiation they had made' (LFF, 1, 98). Williams does not recognize this moment as a glimpse into the future, however, and anticipates few more casualties. This political optimism allows her to celebrate the fact that 'the liberty of twenty-four millions of people will have been purchased at a far cheaper rate than could ever have been expected from the former experience of the world' (LFF, 1, 98). Gothic foreboding, then, is supplanted by images of further commemorations of the fourteenth of July, as the circle of revolutionary spectatorship and sentimental participation widens to embrace future generations of Parisian tourists:

> I fancy I see them pointing out the spot on which the altar of the country stood. I see them eagerly searching for the place where they have heard it recorded, that the National Assembly were seated! I think of these things, and then repeat to myself with transport, 'I was a spectator of the Federation!' (LFF, 1, 109)

Williams' view of the France of the present and the future is shaped by comedic and romance expectations (which might further explain her distaste for Parisian tragedy). Subsequent volumes may foreground the Gothic in their attempt to account for the execution of the king, the violence of the September massacres and the tyranny of the Robespierre regime, but Volume 1, and the early letters of Volume 2, are wedded to more pastoral forms of romance. The episode that Edmund Burke famously turns into a Gothic sensation in his *Reflections*, when the monarch is forced to leave Versailles and the Poissardes demand the presence of Marie-Antoinette, is, in Williams' hands, both an example of popular power and an opportunity to sentimentalize the queen by depicting her as an anxious mother:

> the Queen escaped from her own apartment to the King's...after having remained a few hours concealed in some secret recess of the palace, it was thought proper to comply with the desire of the croud [sic], who repeatedly demanded her presence....
>
> During the whole of the journey from Versailles to Paris, the Queen held the Dauphin in her arms, who had been previously

taught to put his infant hands together, and attempt to soften the enraged multitude by repeating, 'Grâce pour maman!' ['Spare mama!'] (*LFF*, 1, 99)

The image of the suffering mother would be mobilized again in later volumes, as Williams portrays women brought to the scaffold having had their infants torn from their breasts.[12] It is revisited at the end of Volume 1, however, in a more romantic context. The story of the du Fossés, including the 'suffering mother', Monique, with the promise of which Williams teases her correspondent on a number of occasions, provides the denouement to her first revolutionary reflections and an emblem for the transformations wrought by the new wave of feeling.

Williams' acquaintance with the du Fossés began in 1785 when Monique, the daughter-in-law of the tyrannical Baron du Fossé, was in exile in London, and making a living as a French tutor. Monique tells 'the history of her misfortunes, with the pathetic eloquence of her own charming language' and, with her sympathies aroused, Williams records it. Over seven letters, Williams recounts the abuses heaped upon Antoine du Fossé, the Baron's eldest son, as a consequence of his romantic attachment to Monique, a farmer's daughter and companion to Madame du Fossé.

The Baron is an exemplary member of the *ancien régime*:

> Formed by nature for the support of the antient government of France, he maintained his aristocratic rights with unrelenting severity, ruled his feudal tenures with a rod of iron, and considered the lower order of people as a set of beings whose existence was tolerated merely for the use of the nobility. (*LFF*, 1, 115)

Antoine, to the contrary, 'possessed the most amiable of dispositions, and the most feeling heart' (*LFF*, 1, 115), and was a man for whom 'domestic happiness was the first good of life' (*LFF*, 1, 117). He is, that is, the archetype of the new sensibility.

Williams narrates the trials of Antoine and Monique as the perfect revolutionary romance. After their secret marriage, Antoine is subject to a *lettre du cachet*, forced into exile in England, and duped into returning to France only to be imprisoned. Monique, left in England with an infant daughter and little means of support, is an icon of beauty in distress:

she summoned all her strength, and walked with trembling steps to the school where she lived as a teacher. With much difficulty she reached the door; but her limbs could support her no longer, and she fell down senseless at the threshold. (*LFF*, 1, 123)

This scene, like many in the story, would be familiar to readers of sentimental fiction, and Williams self-consciously shapes the account to the expectations of popular romance. But the force and value of the story, she claims, is not its narrative shape but its origin in 'real sufferings':

> when I recollect that I am not at this moment indulging the melancholy cast of my own disposition, by painting imaginary distress; when I recollect not only that these were real sufferings, but that they were sustained by *you*! my mind is overwhelmed with its own sensations – the paper is blotted by my tears – and I can hold my pen no longer. (*LFF*, 1, 119)

Williams' participation in the grief of her friends is meant to distress the reader too, just as the happy denouement, with the death of the Baron and the security afforded the family after the establishment of the National Assembly, provide the romance conclusion the reader would choose: 'Such is the history of Mons du F— . Has it not the air of romance? And are you not glad that the denouement is happy? – Does not the old Baron die exactly in the right place; at the very page one would chuse?' (*LFF*, 1, 139) Historical change under the new regime is directed by popular opinion, a point reiterated in the course of the narrative when, periodically, 'public clamours' (*LFF*, 1, 136) force the Baron and the rest of his family to behave more humanely to Antoine and Monique.

If Williams is a participant in the du Fossés' emotional drama, she shares a more literal performance with them while resident at their chateau near Rouen towards the end of her first journey to France. A *fête* on St Augustin's day provides an opportunity for the family and the Williams sisters to put on a piece called 'La Fédération, ou la Famille Patriotique' for the du Fossés' tenants. Williams takes the role of a statue, 'the representative of liberty' who 'appeared with all her usual attributes, and guarding the consecrated banners of the nation' (*LFF*, 1, 143). Such representations, she notes, bind to the memories of the French the cause of liberty 'and appoint it not merely to regulate the great movements of government, but to mold [sic] the figure of the dance' (*LFF*, 1, 143). Politics and culture come together in the figure of Liberty, here represented by the English woman, Williams.

With such images fresh in her mind, Williams leaves for England, and is dismayed to hear first the derogatory remarks made about the French by the British travellers on the boat and then, back in London, the sensational accounts of the revolution from her acquaintances: 'that every town is the scene of massacre; that every street is blackened with a gallows, and every highway deluged with blood' (*LFF*, 1, 147). It is in part her indignation at these 'misrepresentations' and her desire to give a more favourable view of the revolution that sees Williams return to France in September of the following year, a journey she commemorates in her poem *A Farewell, for Two Years, to England*.[13]

A FAREWELL

The poem, first published in 1791, revives the images of 'Albion' and 'Gallia' – mythologized personifications of England and France – that she used in earlier poetry. The two years that she proposes to absent herself from England are marked by pastoral images: 'twice' returning seasons (ll.7; 9; 11; 13;) 'Spring, dispelling Winter's gloom'(*FE*, l.7); 'village-maids, with chaplets gay,/And simple carols, hail[ing] the return of May' (*FE*, ll.9–10); the 'happy peasants' of autumn who 'bear along/The lavish store, and wake the harvest-song' (*FE*, ll.13–14). It is this 'merry' England that the speaker will recall on her journey. An English-speaking muse will also accompany her:

> Midst foreign sounds, her voice, that charms my ear,
> Breath'd in my native tongue, I still shall hear;
> 'Midst foreign sounds, endear'd will flow the song
> Whose tones, my ALBION, will to thee belong!
>
> (*FE*, ll.61–4)

This muse will prove of greater importance in later volumes of Williams' *Letters*, when, under Robespierre's rule, her sense of being a citizen of the world recedes and she is temporarily imprisoned on the grounds of being a foreigner. Her references to English liberties become more frequent from that point. In this poem, however, the flattering image of her liberal home gives way to criticism of English antagonism to the French revolution. Recalling an image from the first volume of *Letters*, of the English behaving like 'merchants' of liberty and wishing to monopolise 'that precious property' (*FE*, l. 92), she scorns:

> those narrow souls, whate'er their clime,
> Who meanly think that sympathy a crime;
> Who, if one wish for human good expand
> Beyond the limits of their native land,
> And from the worst of ills would others free,
> Deem that warm wish, my Country! Guilt to thee.
>
> (*FE*, ll.87–92)

In this vein, she also revisits the issue of the slave trade, and France's greater progress in its abolition.[14] In Volume 1 of the *Letters*, she had noted how Mirabeau had proposed the abolition of the slave trade to the National Assembly and took the opportunity to scold the English House of Commons for lagging behind and submitting 'to be taught by another nation the lesson of humanity' (*LFF*, 1,84). In *A Farewell*, she reiterates the reprimand to the British government and holds up France as a model of human sympathy:

> oh, since mis'ry, in its last excess,
> In vain from BRITISH honour hopes redress;
> May other Lands the bright example show,
> May other regions lessen human woe!
> Yes, GALLIA, haste! Tho' Britain's sons decline
> The glorious power to save, that power is thine;
>
> (*FE*, ll.181–6)

Having issued her farewell and painted this unflattering comparison between an expansive, liberty-loving France and an inward-looking Britain, the speaker can only hope that when 'the destin'd hour of exile past' and she returns to England hoping to find those she loves, that 'no sharp pang that cherish'd hope destroy,/And from my bosom tear the promis'd joy' (*FE*, ll.207–8). She does not want to find herself exiled in her own country.

Williams may have faced such an ignominious moment when, after the publication of the second volume of *Letters*, she returned to England in June 1792. As hostility to the revolution grew, reviews of her second volume were less favourable than those of the first. She left again for France two months later. With the exception of an interlude in Switzerland in 1794 and a few years in Amsterdam towards the end of her life, Williams' return to France was permanent. That is not to say, however, that Williams did not feel the pains of exile that she describes in *A Farewell*. The shift from monarchical rule to the Convention, and then from the Girondin leader Brissot to the Jacobin Robespierre, saw Williams increasingly alienated from the country with which she had fallen in love. It is this gradual disillusionment with the revolutionary régime – although not with the original revolutionary ideals – that Williams records in the seven volumes of *Letters* published between 1792 and 1796.

SURVEILLANCE AND EXILE

The France that Williams depicts in Volume 1 is urbane and sociable, and with its marketplaces and festivals, popular culture is in the ascendant. The shift in feeling that the revolution has wrought upon the country is emblematized in the history of the du Fossés, narrated as a sentimental romance, but more powerful for its grounding in truth. Romance prevails in Volume 2, as Williams records the dawning of a new 'age of chivalry' (a reference to Burke's claim that, after the revolution, the age of chivalry is dead):

> Living in France at present, appears to me like living in a region of romance. Events the most astonishing are here the occurrences of the day, and every newspaper is filled with articles of intelligence that will form a new era in the history of mankind. The sentiments of the people also are elevated far above the pitch of common life. All the motives which most powerfully stimulate the mind in its ordinary state, seem repressed in consideration of the public good, and every selfish interest is sacrificed with fond alacrity at the altar of the country... I sometimes think that the age of chivalry, instead of being past for ever, is just returned; (*LFF*, 2, 4).

This new age of chivalry in France is signified by the repression of self-interest and the 'consideration of the public good'. The new sensibility of the French is not only more sympathetic but more communal. It is the issue of 'public interest' that eventually leads the new political leaders of France in a direction of social control that is less palatable to Williams: in 1792, the storming of the Tuilleries, the murder of the Swiss guards, and the September massacres; in 1793 the execution of Louis XVI and the declaration of war on Britain and Holland. Even before the Jacobin régime, Williams sees signs of a shift in popular consciousness, from the inclusivity of the days of the *fête*, to a suspicion of those who might not have the interest of the nation at heart. Williams finds herself under such suspicion while watching a procession from a window of the Palais de Bourbon, the former home of Louis Joseph, Prince of Condé, who had fled to England at the beginning of the revolution. The processing crowd turns angrily on the spectators, taunting them as 'aristocratie' (aristocrats). Williams, who once felt herself to be a participant in any public spectacle, recoils from the angry crowd and raises questions about the ability of the 'people' to distinguish their enemies from their allies:

> The people do not reason very logically; and therefore, instead of concluding, as they ought to have done, that since the aristocrats of the Palais de Bourbon were fled, those who remained behind were probably good patriots, their conclusions took quite another turn. They could associate no ideas of patriotism with the Palais de Bourbon, and accused us of aristocracy as they approached. (*LFF*, 2, 145)

The building itself had come to stand for the *ancien régime* and it was later 'nationalized'. This was to be the fate of most Parisian palaces and hotels during the Robespierre years as private wealth was seized for the public good. While Williams and her Gironde friends accepted the principle of more equitable divisions of property, they did not envision the proscriptions that would be placed on commerce and cultural expression in the name of the nation. In Volume 5, Williams records how private profit from commerce was outlawed by the imposition of the 'maximum' (a fixed price for all goods). This standardization was to be echoed in the arts, as Robespierre strove to produce a uniform national culture, and executed a good many of Williams' friends and acquaintances who were deemed to make art for aristocratic rather than popular tastes.

The most direct attack on Williams' freedom came in October 1793, when she and her sister were arrested and imprisoned in the former Luxembourg Palace, before being transferred to the Convent des Anglaises. France was now at war with Britain and the imprisonment of British subjects was part of Robespierre's vengeance for a series of British triumphs in the war. Instead of circulating freely in the openness and 'transparency' of the early revolutionary order, Williams finds herself a victim of the suspicion and scrutiny of Robespierre's régime, under which hiding or being open about one's social origins or allegiances leads to the same end: 'One person was sent to prison, because aristocracy was written in his countenance, another because it was said to be hidden at his heart' (*LFF*, 5, 207). To emphasize the extent of Robespierre's paranoia, Williams describes how not only those deemed to be enemies of the revolution but those whose profession it had been to imitate them – actors and actresses – were condemned by the tyranny of transparency. They had:

> no professional sins to confess, since they had acted their parts on the stage of the world without any disguise. However, the commune thought that those who had been in the habitude of personating princes, and nobles, and queens and countesses, could little relish habits of equality, and therefore sent to prison both actors and actresses as suspected. (*LFF*, 6, 179)

In the later volumes, then, the happy romance has taken a Gothic turn: Robespierre is a malign patriarch ordering things according to his will in the name of the public good and 'the public' is once again divided. Forced into exile in the Convent des Anglaises with other English women, Williams feels herself physically and emotionally divided from the French, and finds comfort in 'the tie of common country' which 'appeared so strong, that it seemed, as Dr Johnson said of family relations, that we were born each others friends' (*LFF*, 5, 186). The English-speaking muse of whom she writes in her *Farewell to England* now provides the solace she anticipated it would. After her release from prison in November 1793, Williams remained in France until the middle of the following year, when the

Committee of Public Safety ordered the nobility and foreigners to leave Paris. She went to Switzerland and stayed there until the end of 1794 when Robespierre's fall made it safe to return. She describes her flight in Gothic terms:

> I proceeded on my journey, haunted by the images of gens d'armes, who I fancied were pursuing me, and with a sort of superstitious persuasion that it was impossible I should escape. I felt as if some magical spell would chain my feet at the frontier of France, which seemed to me a boundary that was impassable. (*LFF*, 5, 174–5)

She did cross the border, and recorded her experience in *A Tour in Switzerland*, first published in 1798, and which I shall address later.

CIVIC RELIGION

Williams' description of Robespierre's Festival of the Supreme Being stands out in the later volumes, as it throws into relief the difference that she perceives between Gironde-led Paris and Jacobin rule. Held in June 1794, just before Williams' departure for Switzerland, the Festival was Robespierre's opportunity to explain his vision of a 'civic religion'. The Festival was rigidly and minutely choreographed by the artist Jacques-Louis David, who, in Williams' eyes 'instead of cherishing that sacred flame of enlightened liberty which is connected with the sublimer powers of the imagination, was the laquey of the tyrant Robespierre' (*LFF*, 6, 74). For Williams, the Festival could not be more different from the Fête de la Fédération, which, although choreographed, was remarkable for the spontaneous and unified emotional response of its spectator-participants:

> Ah, what was then become of those civic festivals, which hailed the first glories of the sublime federation of an assembled nation, which had nobly shaken off its ignominious fetters, and exulted in its newborn freedom! What was become of those moments when no emotions were pre-ordained, no feelings measured out, no acclamations decreed; but when every bosom beat high with admiration, when every heart throbbed with enthusiastic transport, when every eye melted into tears, and the vault of heaven resounded the bursts of un-premeditated applause. (*LFF*, 6, 86)

After the *Fête*, Williams had gleefully imagined future generations commemorating not only the fall of the Bastille, but also the site of its anniversary celebration. Her imagination is more disturbed by the Festival:

> From this profusion of gay objects, which in happier moments would have excited delightful sensations, the drooping soul now turned distasteful. The scent of carnage mingled with these lavish sweets; the glowing festoons appeared tinged with blood; and in the background of this festive scenery the guillotine arose before the disturbed imagination. (*LFF*, 6, 89)

Such 'Gothic' apparitions haunt her throughout Volumes 5 and 6, which chart the days before Robespierre's overthrow in July 1794. For Williams, the light of romance has been extinguished: 'The world has lost its illusive colouring; its fairy spells, its light enchantments have vanished; and death, the idea most familiar to my imagination, appears to my wearied spirit the only point of rest.' (*LFF*, 6, 100)

As befits the heroine of a sentimental and Gothic romance, Williams is granted a reprieve from her despair with the fall of the despot. Volume 7 records the build-up to Robespierre's overthrow and execution, imagined by Williams as apocalypse in reverse:

> Upon the fall of Robespierre, the terrible spell which bound the land of France was broken; the shrieking whirlwinds, the black precipices, the bottomless gulphs, suddenly vanished; and reviving nature covered the wastes with flowers, and the rocks with verdure. (*LFF*, 7, 190)

This image of the return of the pastoral to France is reiterated in the final volume of *Letters*, which records the attempts of the Convention to make reparation for the excesses of Robespierre's régime. Typically, Williams illustrates this restoration of liberty with accounts of communal celebration and domestic happiness. An address from the Convention to the young citizens of Paris, for instance 'produced a sort of electrical effect... They formed themselves into fraternal bands, paraded the streets and public gardens, singing with exulting rapture "Le reveil du people," a popular air' (*LFF*, 8, 24). The return of spontaneous, popular emotion is underpinned by stories of last-minute rescues from the scaffold and she focuses on mothers and fathers restored to their children, couples reunited and families given amnesty for rising against Robespierre.

For Williams, the revolution has reached its conclusion:

> The French republic had now arrived at a pitch of glory unequalled in the annals of modern history The only enemy that France had to dread, was that spirit of savage misrule and anarchy which the demon Jacobinism had raised, and which had transformed the cradle of infant liberty into a den of desolation and carnage. (*LFF*, 8, 127–8)

Jacobinism is a demonic enemy to the revolution, not part of its spirit. It had been Williams' mission to separate the Jacobin from the Gironde in the mind of her British readers. With Robespierre's demise, she hopes that the distinction will become clear:

> history will judge between Brissot and Robespierre...History will not confound those sanguinary and ambitious men who passed along the revolutionary horizon like baneful meteors, spreading destruction in their course, and those whose talents formed a radiant constellation in the zone of freedom, and diffused benignant beams over the hemisphere till extinguished by storms and darkness. (*LFF*, 6, 78)

LETTERS ON THE FEMALE MIND

Although history may well have attended to the difference between one revolutionary regime and another, Williams' contemporaries in Britain seem not to have. Along with the predictable reactions of the conservative press to Williams' continuing support for the revolution, a number of friends and acquaintances, including Hester Piozzi and Anna Seward, distanced themselves from her. Hostility to the style of the *Letters*, as well as to their political sympathies, grew, and Williams stood charged with conflating history with fiction. The most extended criticism that Williams received along these lines was from a literary acquaintance, Laetitia Matilda Hawkins, whose two-volume *Letters on the Female Mind* (1793) were addressed 'to Miss H. M. Williams, With particular reference to her Letters from France'.[15] Hawkins attacks Williams for her 'Gallic prejudice' and her sympathies with the French 'mob', but she reserves her most critical voice for Williams' blend of romance and reality:

> do not let us imagine that the fairies and sprites of our fancy are terrestrial beings, that by our travels in the land of fiction we gain knowledge of the *human heart*, or that a world where every species of corruption has been increasing during ages, is to be now, by a sudden change of principles, regulated by pastoral simplicity.[16]

The force of Hawkins' critique implies that she was anxious that Williams would win over the hearts of British readers to the revolutionary cause through her narrative technique. Williams' Manichean portraits of the *ancien régime* and the members of the National Assembly, of Girondists and Jacobins, her sentimental vignettes of victims of the pre-revolutionary order and, more powerfully, of her friends who died at the hands of Robespierre, are offered in a broader frame of the dawn, suspension and return of the light of romance, and Hawkins objects to this seductive narrative arc. Further, whilst the bound volumes of Williams' *Letters* were destined for a limited readership, extracts were reprinted in newspapers and periodicals and found their way to a broader – if not quite 'popular' – audience in a way that was bound to alarm reactionary commentators like Hawkins.

Williams' *Letters from France* are not 'confessional' memoirs. We learn little, for instance, of her relationship with John Hurford Stone, of the illness that struck her down in 1792, or her anxiety about the alienation of her friends back in England. The *Letters* are written in the spirit of a long epistolary tradition of 'intimate', but public, correspondence, which was itself turned into fiction in the eighteenth century, so that by the 1790s letters teem with recognizable tropes from novels as well as other traditions of letter writing.[17] Williams constructs a particular persona for her correspondent: the political *ingénue*, moved by a revolution in human sentiment. This *ingénue* is at times the revolution's participant, temporarily its victim and latterly its champion in the face of much opposition. Williams spent much of the remainder of her writing career vindicating her loyalty to the revolution and her decision to remain in France until she died in 1827. One such vindication went into print before the end of the 1790s. Her *Tour in Switzerland*, inspired by her period in exile from the Jacobin regime in 1794, was written in 1797 and published a year later, and charts her ongoing enthusiasm for the spirit of French enlightenment, indeed her desire for it to move west to Switzerland, even in her darkest days of exile from her adopted *patrie*.

9

Sublime Exile: *A Tour in Switzerland*

In the middle of 1794, during the Reign of Terror, Robespierre's grip on the revolutionary regime was at its tightest, although he soon succumbed to the guillotine when another faction came to the fore. This was no time for associates of the Girondins, like Williams, to be in Paris, and with the help of the man assumed to be her lover, John Hurford Stone, she fled to Switzerland. *A Tour in Switzerland* was not written until 1797, and was published a year later.[1] By then, Williams was back in France and the country was under the more moderate regime of the Directory. As in her *Letters*, so in the *Tour*, Williams could look back and see the Reign of Terror as a dark, regressive episode in an otherwise enlightened process of revolutionary change, although it was popularly viewed as the worst excess of a bloody and violent period of French history.

While the chance to contextualize this period was one political motivation for the composition of the *Tour*, there was another reason. In 1797, what Williams in her Preface to the *Tour* would call 'the electrical fire' of revolution was about to release its 'subtle spark' and ignite its neighbour Switzerland (*TS*, 1, 4); Bonaparte (later emperor Napoleon) was about to invade. This was a timely moment to comment on the necessity for change in Switzerland. While she would join in the tradition of other published travellers to Switzerland by sketching its 'sublime scenery', Williams claims the originality of her *Tour* lies in her observations of the 'present moral situation of Switzerland' (*TS*, 1, 3) and a comparison with the present state of France. As we have seen in her poetry and her *Letters*, Williams was influenced by the 'philosophical historians' like Gibbon, Hume and

Robertson, who were motivated to show the influence of customs and manners in shaping the fortunes of nations. The *Tour* is as much part of that tradition as it is part of a tradition of travel writing. Indeed, Gibbon wrote, but never published, two volumes of a history of Switzerland that celebrated the old Swiss struggle for independence. Gibbon was critical, though, of contemporary Swiss politics and the aristocratic republics. To some degree, Williams' *Tour* completes Gibbon's projected history, outlining the fall of Swiss liberty but projecting its imminent return.

LITERARY TOURISTS

Switzerland was a popular stopping point on the eighteenth-century Grand Tour and was remarked upon for its natural beauty and for its political liberty. Those who had 'trodden before' the paths that Williams 'delighted to tread', and who would publish their findings, included William Coxe, whose *Sketches of the Natural, Civil, and Political State of Switzerland* (1779) would be a guide for travellers and a source for other writers, most famously William Wordsworth and later Byron and Shelley. The 1790s were obviously difficult years for the polite traveller, and many British tourists turned to their own rural beauty spots until continental Europe was a safer destination. Others who published their travels of Switzerland in the 1790s did so with their eyes firmly on the scenery, or commented on the politics only to deride the signs of republican spirit that Williams celebrated.[2] Williams, then, was in an unusual position: she was a female traveller; she was a Briton still in Europe in the 1790s; she was a Briton in Europe whose political sympathies still lay with republicanism.

Williams was not travelling at leisure, but under duress. The psychological pressures of her journey often reveal themselves in the physical difficulties of ascending mountains or traversing rivers. Her ascent to the glaciers, for instance, is 'a journey of extreme toil' (*TS*, 2, 5). Forced to leave behind the mule that has so far been her travel escort, she suffers the effects of heat and altitude. While she is restored to tranquillity (and quotes Rousseau on the serenity of the mountains to prove her point) she sits down while her companions 'amused themselves by wandering over a world of ice' (*TS*, 2, 8). She is composed enough on her frozen seat to employ 'the hours of meditation in throwing together the new images with which the Alpine scenery had filled my mind, into the form of an hymn, to the author of nature' (*TS*, 2, 10). She appends 'A Hymn Written among the Alps' to Volume 2. The poem hints at the alarm Williams evidently experienced, as she alludes to the 'stern' Alpine mountains, the 'sharp rock' and the 'slippery summit', but she contains these anxieties in the poem's devotional rhetoric, finding signs of divinity in the most threatening of scenes:

> In every scene, where every hour
> Sheds some terrific grace,
> In nature's vast, overwhelming power,
> THEE, THEE, my God, I trace!
>
> (ll.396–400)

The meditative calm of the poem belies the alarm of her situation, as first her companions go out of view, and then her mule escapes his tether. Unable to walk unaided, Williams has the guides make a chair to carry her back down the mountainside. When she refers later to the 'regions of stupendous greatness' 'the thrill of astonishment' and 'the transport of adoration' she felt on achieving such height, she misses out the details of terror, the uncertainty, the isolation and the fatigue. The tranquil sublime of 'A Hymn Written Among the Alps' owes more, then, to her late-night reflection than to her daytime difficulties, and anticipates Wordsworth's edict of 1800 that poetry is 'emotion recollected in tranquility'.

The reference to Rousseau's account of the glaciers is one of many acknowledgements of Williams' 'sources' for her journey. When Williams recounts her arrival in Switzerland she lays bare her preconceptions, shaped by reading Coxe and Rousseau. To emphasize the second-hand nature of her expectations, Williams 'quotes' her initial response to the Swiss sublime:

> The first view of Switzerland awakened my enthusiasm most powerfully – 'At length,' thought I, 'am I going to contemplate that interesting country, of which I have never heard without emotion! – I am going to gaze upon images of nature; images of which the idea has so often swelled my imagination' (*TS*, 1, 4)

Williams' tendency to 'self-quotation' complicates the first-person voice of the *Tour*. She is at pains to acknowledge the 'sources' that have shaped her expectations and her experience of the landscape. When faced with the task of writing about the glaciers, Williams at first defers to Ramond de Carbonnieres' *Observations on the Glacieres*, putting an annotated translation of the essay in the appendix to her *Tour*; she then allows Rousseau to speak for her. Rousseau looms large in the country around Vevay, evidenced when she encounters a scene that he rendered in fiction, in *La Nouvelle Hêloïse*, and that has subsequently been lived out by literary tourists:

> It would be hopeless to attempt a new sketch of these enchanting regions after the glowing description of Rousseau, which has already been so often detailed by the hundred sentimental pilgrims, who, with Heloise in hand, run over the rocks and mountains to catch the lover's inspiration. (*TS*, 2, 179)

Williams is not the sentimental pilgrim she was in 1790, and nor is the scene before her able to conjure the same sentimental response in her that Rousseau's description evoked: 'All in nature is still romantic, wild, and graceful, as Rousseau has painted it; but the soothing charm associated with the moral feeling, is in some sort dissolved' (*TS*, 2, 179). The 'soothing charm associated with the moral feeling' is dissolved because of the degraded state of Switzerland, and, perhaps, because of Williams' experiences in France. She arrives in Switzerland much more jaded than she appeared on her arrival in Paris. While initially the landscape 'fulfilled the glowing promise of imagination', several weeks' residence at Basle 'chilled [her] enthusiasm' for the character of the people (*TS*, 1, 5), as she found them mercenary and philistine. When Williams cites Coxe, it is no surprise that it is partly to undo his dominant argument about the liberty of Switzerland. She finds an unusually negative comment of his on the town of Lucerne 'of all places in Switzerland, that in which literature is the least encouraged and cultivated'. She confirms and updates his comment, noting that 'this town contains not one bookseller's shop' but that she found a 'select society of men of letters devoting their time to those researches which were most likely to prove beneficial to their country' (*TS*, 2, 119). The enlightened literary men are avatars of greater liberty spreading from France and restored from a former Switzerland:

> Although the liberty of the press, the palladium of all other liberty, is universally proscribed in Switzerland, neither the force of authority, nor the imprimatur of a censor, have been able to impede the gradual progress of that knowledge which will lead to freedom unsullied by anarchy or violence, and restore to this country its antient renown. (*TS*, 2, 120–1)

FRENCH ENLIGHTENMENT

While the description of bookshop-free Lucerne is unusual in Coxe's largely celebratory account of Switzerland, in Williams' version it is a typical sign of a culture oppressed by an aristocratic oligarchy on the verge of (re)enlightenment. Invariably in the *Tour*, enlightenment spreads from the west, from France. It is part of Williams' expressed purpose to compare the Swiss cantons with the French republic, or more particularly Paris, and to justify the imminent French invasion. From early in Volume 1, a picture is sketched of a stolid, dour Swiss and a vivacious, libidinous French populace. While the 'burghers of Basil' [sic] pursue their trade without relief, 'since even the hours of relaxation are made subservient to the views of interest' (*TS*, 1, 7), the French have a 'sort of rage for commerce', animated 'not only by the call of necessity, but by the desire of enjoyment' (*TS*, 1, 18). The women of Basle are locked in dull routine and conversation amounts to 'the domestic detail of household anecdote, and the tattle of town scandal' (*TS*, 1, 12). It comes as little surprise that Williams describes the women of France, who 'have even more active spirits than the men', as enthusiastic entrepreneurs or powerful 'agents and emissaries of their friends, lovers, or husbands, in the public offices' (*TS*, 1, 25). These women, 'the most beautiful, and the most intriguing of the fair Parisians' (*TS*, 1, 25), took up roles in the 'marine, the war, and the home-departments' and, according to Williams, brought to the republican committees the same 'formidable artillery of bright eyes, gay smiles, lively sallies, and animated graces' that women brought to the polished courts of the *ancien régime* (*TS*, 1, 25). For Williams, femininity remains in the ascendancy in revolutionary France.

Given that Williams is looking back to 1794, when France was experiencing the worst atrocities of the Jacobin regime, she would be hard-pressed to find unqualified praise for the country from which she has recently been exiled. Even for an apologist like Williams, there is a threatening undercurrent in the disposition of the 'impetuous French', and she struggles to represent the transition from monarchy to Robespierre and beyond in a positive light. As she describes the entrepreneurial energy of the French, then, she must note the losses as well as the gains, exemplified in the transformation of monasteries into factories: 'No doubt an artisan is far more useful than a monk, but he looks much less picturesque when placed beneath a ruined arch, and gazed at in perspective.' (*TS*, 1, 22)

While the picturesque has been sacrificed to utility in France, Williams is quick to assert that not all pleasure has been resigned to principle. Urbanity still reigns in Paris, evidenced by the 'two-thousand ball-rooms of the capital' which prove that 'no revolution has taken place in the manners of the French, and that they are still a dancing nation' (*TS*, 1, 29). The darkness of the Robespierre regime later clouds this observation, however, as she describes the trend, in the winter of 1793, to hold 'bals a la victime', subscription balls held in memory of the those who died in the Terror and open to 'any person with a certificate of their execution in his pocket-book' (*TS*, 1, 41).

RELIGIOUS REVIVALISM

Despite her overriding tendency to defend the revolutionary regime, Williams does caricature what she sees as revolutionary fashions, such as the religious revivals of the mid 1790s, which were characteristic of the unstable Jacobin period. While many 'wearied with revolutionary calamities' returned to the Catholic Church's 'soothing consolations of devotion', the 'fine ladies and gentlemen' of Paris went back to the Church because 'infidelity' was now 'profaned by the vulgar Jacobin touch' (*TS*, 1, 73-6). No sooner had Catholicism become the fashion among the Parisian *ton*, however, than the 'butterfly tribe' (*TS*, 1, 78) found another sect, and then another.[3] With such 'coarse impiety' in Paris, Williams finds relief in the 'respectful demeanour and devout attention' of the French Protestant worshippers in Basle.

In all other ways, though, the populace of Basle are found wanting in comparison with their Parisian neighbours. The peasantry, the manufacturers and the burghers are all in a degraded state compared with their post-revolutionary French counterparts. The fickle religious revivalism of the Parisian *ton* may be a subject for derision, but Williams finds a religious tolerance in France that is lacking in Switzerland, citing examples of anti-Semitism and a prohibition on Catholicism in the Protestant canton of Basle. For Williams, this is the prejudice of the unenlightened, fuelled by a decline in scholarship:

> we are told by Mr Cox, that he found shopkeepers in this city [Basle] reading Virgil, Horace, and Plutarch; from which he was, no doubt, well authorized to draw his conclusion, that there is no country in the world where the people are so happy. But whatever were the Halcyon days of taste and learning at the period of Mr Cox's visit, it is a melancholy fact, that this literary spirit has entirely evaporated since his departure. (TS, 1, 114–15)

Part of Williams' agenda in the *Tour* is to chart the demise of Swiss scholarship and enlightenment, but also to predict its resurrection at the hands of the French. Basle, she anticipates 'will, from its moral and geographical position, be the first to cast away its shroud' (TS, 1, 119) (borrowing an expression from Gibbon). The resurrection will, according to Williams, be engineered by Bonaparte. As Nigel Leask suggests, Napoleon Bonaparte, not the Alps, evokes the real sublime in the *Tour*.[4] For Williams, the transcendent Bonaparte is of, but not confined to, the French Revolution, and will cast his light on Switzerland.

If Bonaparte is one source of the sublime in the *Tour*, the revolution is another. Williams brings together the topographical and political sublime in the following image of a traveller ascending a mountain:

> Like the traveller, who from the scorching plains, climbs the rocks that lead him to the regions of eternal snow, and finds that in the space of a few hours he has passed through every successive latitude, from burning heat to the confines of the frozen pole, the journey of months; so the human mind, placed within the sphere of the French Revolution, has bounded over the ruggedness of slow metaphysical researches, and reached at once, with an incredible

effort, the highest probable attainment of political discovery. (*TS*, 2, 270–1)

We have seen already how Williams struggled with such an ascent, only to look back on it as a journey that gave her access to the sublime. The comparison, then with her experience of the revolution, the rapidity of change, and its physical and psychical discomfort, is fitting.

VIRTUE IN DISTRESS

As in the later volumes of the *Letters*, so in the *Tour*, Williams extends her sympathies to the revolutionary exiles. Another episode involving the difficulties of travelling, when Williams finds herself separated from her companions while darkness encroaches, leads to a chance encounter with an exiled French aristocrat, Mme de C—, who has taken residence in a cottage outside Bellinzone. In the ensuing history that Mme de C recounts, 'which she probably saw I was anxious to know, more from a sentiment of sympathy, than a principle of curiosity' (*TS*, 1, 286), she reveals herself as a woman of similar mind to Williams. The daughter of a French nobleman, she married an opponent of the revolution, but her 'enlarged mind exulted in that change of system which she dared not openly applaud ...and was more disposed to rejoice in the amelioration of solid substantial wretchedness, than to lament the ideal deprivations of greatness' (*TS*, 1, 288). Her less principled husband emigrates from France, leaving her behind to protect their property until the 'counter-revolution arrived' (*TS*, 1, 289). When the counter-revolution fails to arrive, Mme de C follows her husband, only to discover that he has fallen for the charms of a renowned Parisian salonnière, Madame de — 'a Parisian lady of high rank, who had been distinguished in the ancient regime for the brilliancy of her coteries, and the number of her adorers' (*TS*, 1, 299). The revolution brought this period to an end, however. It:

> dispersed her adorers, transformed Paris into a new region, where the altars of pleasure were overthrown, where incense was offered at the shrine of a new goddess, and where Madame de — was stunned from morning til night with the enthusiastic acclamations of the

vulgar, whom she had been accustomed to consider as born of slavery and silence; (*TS*, 1, 301)

Madame de — is a victim of the rapidly shifting, quasi-religious, sensibilities of the Parisians in the 1790s. True to the entrepreneurial spirit of Parisian women which Williams catalogued earlier in the *Tour*, Madame de — finds herself a young nobleman, furnishes herself with his money and a false passport, and sets off for Switzerland. Dispensing with the nobleman, she comes upon M. de C—, who quickly succumbs to her charms. Meanwhile his wife is reduced to taking in embroidery to pay for her lodgings, and keep her maid and child. Mme de C— shows a different kind of entrepreneurialism when she embraces her humble labour:

> To have the power of applying those accomplishments, which she had only cultivated as the amusement of a solitary hour, to the dear, the precious purpose of sustaining her child, filled her mind with the sweetest sensations of maternal tenderness – it was delight, elevated by the noble consciousness of duty – (*TS*, 1, 313)

Virtue in this instance is rewarded, and a penitent M. de C— is reunited with his wife. The family live together in post-revolutionary domestic bliss 'which, to a sensibility like hers, is the first of blessings; she has a mind capable of relinquishing rank and splendor without a sigh, since she has found happiness in exchange' (*TS*, 1, 321–2). Like the sentimental vignettes in the *Letters*, Mme de C—'s story is a morality tale for the French aristocracy: the enlightened Mme de C— triumphs over her decadent peer and exerts her moral influence to reform her wayward husband too.

A JOURNEY TO FRANCE

Williams leaves the family still in exile. She, however, returns to Paris, 'with feelings how different from those I had felt on my departure! I had now only scenes of gratulation to witness, and only tears of luxury to shed!' (*TS*, 2, 278). She returns, that is, to a different regime, one that is to extend its vision to Switzerland. Williams' optimism about Bonaparte and the enlightenment of Switzerland was not shared by her reviewers, particularly after the French invasion proved violent. Just as Williams had been vilified for her marriage of politics and sensibility, history and romance in her *Letters*, so reviewers object to her commentary on the Swiss government. *The Monthly Review*, for instance, commends her responses to the Swiss landscape, the poetry of her descriptions, but cannot tolerate her presumption to write on politics: 'Politics seem to be Miss Williams's favourite science, but it is not the subject in which she is the best qualified to excel'. Less predictably, the *Monthly* reviewer locates this weakness not in Williams' gender but in her poetic disposition, with which she keeps surprising company: 'The late Mr Burke, in his far-famed pamphlet, ridicules with great vivacity the geometrical politicians of France: but both he and Miss Williams afford very striking examples that poetical politicians are not less objectionable.'[5]

Despite the criticism which must have been predictable to Williams by now, she remained open in her optimism about and support for the French Republic, and in 1801 published her two-volume *Sketches of the Manners and Opinions of the French Republic*. Now under the leadership of Napoleon Bonaparte, France still looked to Williams like a beacon of liberty, although she does criticize the violence used against Switzerland. This year was to be a turning-point in Williams' writing career and in her relationship with the Napoleonic regime. As she recalls in her Preface to her 1823 volume of poetry, 1801 saw the publication of her (second) 'Ode on the Peace' in the *Morning Chronicle*, which was inspired by the treaty signed between the English and France that year. The poem, she remembers, brought Williams under the scrutiny of Napoleon:

> The only memorable circumstance in the history of this Ode is its having incurred the displeasure of Buonaparte [sic]: he found it in a corner of the Morning Chronicle, and it was translated into French by his order. He pretended to be highly irritated at the expression 'encircled by thy subject-waves,' applied to England, and which he said was treasonable towards France; but what he really resented was, that his name was not once pronounced in the Ode.[6]

Under Napoleon's rule, first as First Consul from 1799 and five years later as Emperor, until his abdication and exile in 1814, French literature was heavily censored. Williams wrote little during these years, although she remained at the centre of

Parisian cultural life, coming back to the public eye with her translations of the work of the German explorer Alexander von Humboldt.[7] Two accounts of the Restoration of Louis XVIII and its aftermath and a complaint on the persecution of Protestants see Williams resume her commentary on French politics.[8]

In 1823, some thirty-seven years since the publication of her two-volume *Poems*, Williams published *Poems on Various Subjects*, having 'long renounced any attempts in verse, confining my pen almost entirely to sketches of the Revolution' (*Poems VS*, ix). The collection looks back across her poetic career and includes a number of poems not published elsewhere, as well as edited and revised versions of early work. In her Introduction, Williams classifies only four of the poems as relating to public events (*Peru*, *A Poem on the Bill passed for regulating the Slave Trade*, 'The Bastille' and *Ode on the Peace*), and she makes a distinction between the authority of her attempts to tread 'on the territory of History' in her prose narratives which 'make a part of that marvelous story which the eighteenth century has to record to future times' (*Poems VS*, x) and these 'slight compositions' which 'scarcely deserve the honours of a grave defence' (*Poems VS*, ix). In her own terms, she gives the collection more gravity by devoting part of the introduction to a defence of the state of science and literature in France, responding again to criticism levelled from her home country.

There is a more self-conscious separation of public and private in her later poetry than in her earlier efforts. There are a number of poems addressed to her nephews, Athanase and Charles Coquerel, the sons of her sister Cecilia who died in 1798 when the boys were just three years and eighteen months old respectively. Williams, her mother, and sister Persis took over their care. 'Verses addressed to my Two Nephews, on Saint Helen's Day, 1809', published in Paris in that year, presents a glimpse of Williams in the maternal role she took on after 1798. There is a sense in other poems from these years of Williams 'at home', albeit in the 'public' home of the salon, being visited by the great and the good. A number of poems, for instance, are prompted by the receipt of flowers (from an anonymous friend, from author James Forbes and from Humboldt); another by the gift of a Christmas plum pudding. Even in this quasi-retired posture, however, Williams allows the public to infiltrate the private, most notably in the poem written on the occasion of her nephew Athanase's wedding. 'The Charter' playfully uses the political analogy of the French Charter to advise her nephew on his duty as a properly enlightened husband.

The glimpses of Williams' maternal role in these poems are the closest she comes to self-revelation in her literary texts. While the *Letters*, the *Tour* and her later writings on the Restoration are all written as personal recollections, they are not personal memoirs. Her final publication, the *Souvenirs de la révolution française* is offered as a memoir, but looks at the public rather than the private events of Williams' lifetime. The most telling silence is on her relationship with John Hurford Stone, although her hostile reviewers filled the gaps with their own prurient speculations. Unlike her peer Charlotte Smith, Williams is not a Romantic autobiographer in that she does not foreground her own mental progress, personal development or state of being in her writing. The opacity with which she refers to herself in her texts places her in another era. She is aware of the almost quaint classicism when in 1823, she asks her English readers to indulge her 'strangeness':

> considered as a stranger in England (although my heart throbs at its name), my portion of indulgence will perhaps be scanty. My literary patrons belonged to 'the days of other years,' when a ray of favour sometimes fell on my early essays in verse. I can now only expect that, it being the nature of the English public to be just, I shall meet with no more severity than I deserve. (*Poems VS*, xiv)

Williams died in Paris in 1827. For many years the reading public responded with indifference rather than severity to her writing. It took, perhaps, the bicentennial of the French revolution in 1989 and the broadening of interest in the writers of the turn of the nineteenth century who are not strictly Romantics to revive critical interest in Williams. To come to terms with Williams' writing, one must not confuse the sentimental with the confessional, the first-person voice with the autobiographical subject. Williams is not a 'Romantic' in the sense that Charlotte Smith arguably is. But by its difference her writing sheds light on the particularity of Romanticism and on our need to look beyond it if we are to fully understand the literary culture of the late eighteenth and early nineteenth centuries.

Afterword

The works of Charlotte Smith and Helen Maria Williams share a historical moment and a cultural context. Broadly liberal in their treatment of key political issues on the 1780s to the early 1800s (and beyond for Williams), their rhetoric is at times boldly revolutionary, at others, uncertain, disillusioned and despairing. Williams and Smith understand the language and transformative powers of sensibility, and the significance of subjective experience and of moral adjudication in the representation of history. They each make a case for bringing women's perspectives into public life, by virtue of lives that have more enforced 'privacy' than men's, and to use such perspectives to effect change in the moral, as well as the political, landscape.

Both women become sceptical of the ideal of social transparency that was such a positive force for change at the beginning of the French revolution. This scepticism was inflected partly by the revolution's turn to Terror, but also by their awareness of women's different experiences of changing social mores. Both Smith and Williams recognized that they lived in a culture that had more exacting standards for women than for men in terms of their interior morality, and that women had more to lose by self-revelation and 'transparent' conduct.

This distrust of transparency may be one reason why the relationship between the lives and the works of these women is not straightforward. I have emphasized throughout this book the 'mediated' character of both women's self-representations. While Smith is recognized for her autobiographical presence in many of her texts, it is a performative, rather than a directly expressive, presence. It is more dominant, too, at the beginning of her writing career than at the end, in the *Elegiac Sonnets* more than in *Beachy Head*. The trajectory of Williams' self-representation goes in the opposite direction. The third-person speakers of the early, mannered poetry gives way to the first-person narrator of the *Letters from France* and the Swiss *Tour*; still, however, there is little autobiographical disclosure or reflection in her work, until hints at an interior life come to the fore in the later poetry of the 1820s. Whether Williams lost the fear of self-disclosure after the death of Stone, and Smith tired of self-revelation, we can only speculate. However, we can make no easy correlation between biographical events and their textual representation.

Smith capitalizes on this gap between self and work, and manufactures a performative and reflective consciousness in her texts that is by turn satirical, meditative and querulous. This is what makes her 'Romantic'. The voices of Williams' texts are equally performative, from the intertextuality of the early poems, the self-conscious interplay of romance and historical narrative in the *Letters from France*, to the self-quotation, and second-hand tourism of the *Tour in Switzerland*. In Williams' work, however, there is not the sustained, self-revisionary consciousness that we find in Smith's texts. Williams maintains an enlightenment faith in narrative and the progress that it maps, and places less emphasis than her peer on the provisionality of the narrating voice. That this makes her less 'Romantic' than Smith does not make her work less valuable. Williams reminds us that not all British writers of this period, not even the progressives and the revolutionaries, were Romantics, and throws more light on our understanding of that term because of her difference.

Notes

INTRODUCTION

1. *The Works of Charlotte Smith*, General Editor Stuart Curran, 14 vols (London: Pickering and Chatto, 2005–7); *The Collected Letters of Charlotte Smith*, ed. by Judith Phillips Stanton (Bloomington and Indianapolis: Indiana University Press, 2003); *Celestina*, ed. by Loraine Fletcher (Ontario: Broadview Press, 2004); *Emmeline* ed. by Loraine Fletcher (Ontario: Broadview Press, 2003); *Desmond*, ed. by Antje Blank and Janet Todd (Ontario: Broadview, 2001); *The Old Manor House*, ed. by Jaqueline M. Labbe (Ontario: Broadview Press, 2002); Loraine Fletcher, *Charlotte Smith: A Critical Biography* (Basingstoke: Palgrave, 1998).
2. Recounted in the *Patriote françois*, 21 November 1792, cited by Stuart Curran, 'Charlotte Smith and British Romanticism', Creating a Literary Series: The Brown University Women Writers Project and the Oxford University Press 'Women Writers in English, 1350–1850' Texts, *South Central Review*, 11:2 (Summer 1994), 66–78, p.69.
3. Richard Polwhele, *The Unsex'd Females: A Poem, Addressed to the Author of the Pursuits of Literature* (London: Cadell, 1798).
4. *The Poems of Charlotte Smith*, ed. by Stuart Curran (New York: Oxford University Press, 1993), 5.
5. *European Magazine*, 9 (1786), 366.
6. *Critical Review*, 9 (1793), 299–300.
7. Walter Scott, 'Charlotte Smith', *Miscellaneous Prose Works*, 4 (Edinburgh: Cadell, 1834), 125.
8. Theresa M. Kelly, 'Romantic Histories: Charlotte Smith and *Beachy Head*', *Nineteenth-Century Literature*, 59:3 (December 2004), 281–314, p. 285. See Stuart Curran, 'Charlotte Smith and British Romanticism', Creating a Literary Series: The Brown University Women Writers Project and the Oxford University Press 'Women Writers in English, 1350–1850' Texts, *South Central Review*, 11:2 (Summer 1994), 66–78; Jacqueline M. Labbe, *The Culture of Gender: Charlotte Smith, Poetry, and Romanticism* (Manchester: Manchester University Press,

2003); Sarah M. Zimmerman, 'Varieties of Privacy in Charlotte Smith's Poetry', *European Romantic Review*, 18:4 (October 2007), 483–502.
9. Helen Maria Williams, *Letters Written in France, In the Summer 1790, to a Friend in England; containing various anecdotes relative to the French Revolution*, ed. by Neil Fraistat and Susan S. Lanser (Ontario: Broadview Press, 2001).
10. *The Analytical Review* (December 1790), 431; *The General Magazine* (December 1790), 541-3; *Universal Magazine* (December 1790), 289.
11. *The Analytical Review* (December 1790), 431.
12. *The General Magazine* (December 1790), 542.
13. *The Anti-Jacobin*, 36 (9 July, 1798); the poem was accompanied by a print of the same name by Gillray.
14. *A Tour in Switzerland; or, A View of the Present State of the Governments and Manners of those Cantons: with Comparative Sketches of the Present State of Paris*, 2 vols (London: Robinson, 1798), vol. 1, 78.
15. *The Anti-Jacobin Review and Magazine*, 1, 146–7.
16. Laetitia Matilda Hawkins, *Letters on the Female Mind, Its Powers and Pursuits. Addressed to Miss H.M. Williams, With particular reference to her 'Letters' from France*, 2 vols (London: Hookham and Carpenter, 1793).
17. See Steven Blakemore, 'Revolution and the French Disease: Laetitia Matilda Hawkins's Letters to Helen Maria Williams', *Studies in English Literature, 1500–1900*, 36:3 (1996), 673–91 for a fuller discussion of this issue.
18. M. Ray Adams, 'Helen Maria Williams and the French Revolution', *Wordsworth and Coleridge: Studies in Honor of George McLean Harper*, ed. by Earle Leslie Griggs (Princeton: Princeton University Press, 1939), 87–117, p.91 and p.99.
19. See Mary Favret, *Romantic Correspondence: Women, Politics and the Fiction of Letters* (Cambridge: Cambridge University Press, 1993); Vivien Jones, 'Women Writing Revolution: Narratives of History and Sexuality in Wollstonecraft and Williams', in *Beyond Romanticism: New Approaches to Texts and Contexts, 1780-1832*, ed. by Stephen Copley and John Whale, 1780–1832 (London: Routledge, 1992), 178-99; Angela Keane, 'Helen Maria Williams's *Letters from France*: A National Romance', *Prose Studies* 15 (1992), 271–94 and *Women Writers and the English Nation in the 1790s: Romantic Belongings* (Cambridge: Cambridge University Press, 2000); Deborah Kennedy, 'Benevolent Historian: Helen Maria Williams and Her British Readers', in Adriana Craciun and Kari E. Lokke (eds.), *Rebellious Hearts: British Women Writers and the French Revolution* (Albany, NY: SUNY, 2001), 317–36.
20. *Poems on Various Subjects. With Introductory Remarks on the Present*

NOTES

State of Science and Literature in France (London: Whittaker, 1823), pp. xii–xiii.
21. Wordsworth's note to 'Stanzas Suggested in a Steamboat off Saint Bees' Heads', *The Poetical Works of William Wordsworth*, ed. by Ernest de Selincourt and Helen Darbishire, 5 vols (Oxford: Clarendon Press, 1949), vol. 4, 403.
22. *Souvenirs de la révolution française*, trans. from English by Charles Coquerel (Paris: Doney-Dupré, 1827), 198–9.

CHAPTER 1. AN UNFINISHED WORK: CHARLOTTE SMITH'S *ELEGIAC SONNETS*

1. *Elegiac Sonnets, and Other Poems* (London: Dodlsey, 1784). Citations in this chapter refer to *The Poems of Charlotte Smith*, ed. by Stuart Curran (Oxford: Oxford University Press, 1993), abbreviated to Curran.
2. Stuart Curran, *Poetic Form and British Romanticism* (Oxford: Oxford University Press, 1986), 29.
3. Collins, Otway, Hayley and Sargent make up a 'Sussex school' of writers, a group in which Smith implicitly places herself. Many of the sonnets draw on the landscape of the South Downs, the environs of the River Arun and the cliff tops along the Sussex coast. Her affinity with them is not just geographical. Collins's poor mental health and Otway's abject poverty make them particularly sympathetic subjects for Smith.
4. Smith sold the contents of her library several years before she died to address pressing financial demands.
5. Smith's father-in-law, Richard Smith, died in 1776, leaving a large estate and a labyrinthine will, couched in terms that were meant to prevent his profligate son getting his hands on money intended for his grandchildren. The will was so complicated, however, that it was not settled until after Charlotte's death 23 years later. Smith blamed the trustees of the estate for the interminable delay: '"Honorable Men" who, nine years ago, undertook to see that my family obtained the provision their grandfather designed for them... But still I am condemned to feel the "hope delayed that maketh the heart sick"' (Curran, 5).
6. In her essay 'Thorns and Roses: the Sonnets of Charlotte Smith', *Women's Writing*, 2:1 (1995), 43–53, Deborah Kennedy attempts to find a coherent autobiographical persona in the sonnets, at least in those not based on Petrarch's sonnets, Goethe's *Werther* or the sonnets attributed to characters in Smith's novels. Kennedy reads

the remaining sonnets as both record of Smith's biographical woes and a therapeutic outlet for them.
7. Jacqueline M. Labbe, *The Culture of Gender: Charlotte Smith, Poetry, and Romanticism* (Manchester: Manchester University Press, 2003), 112.
8. The full title of Young's poem is *The Complaint, or Night Thoughts on Life, Death and Immortality*.
9. Loraine Fletcher, *Charlotte Smith: A Critical Biography* (Basingstoke: Palgrave, 1998), 53.
10. *Celestina*, penned by the heroine (Sonnets 49–53); *The Old Manor House*, in the voice of Orlando Somerive (Sonnets 61–2); *The Banished Man*, written by Mrs Denzil (Sonnet 64); *Montalbert* by Sommers Walsingham (Sonnets 66–7); *Marchmont* by Edward-Armyn Marchmont (Sonnet 76) and *The Young Philosopher* by Mrs Glenmorris, Delmont and Elisabeth Lisburne (Sonnets 85–7).
11. The tone here could not be more different to that of an earlier poem, Sonnet 18, 'To The Earl of Egremont', which is a paean to Sir George O'Brien, Earl of Egremont, who was renowned for his artistic patronage. Smith turned to Egremont for support with respect to her children's trust in the late 1790s.
12. The historian Bryan Edwards, a champion of Smith's work, encouraged Smith to approach the publisher Richard Dodsley with her *Elegiac Sonnets*. William Hayley agreed to be the 'dedicatee' of the first edition; his name helped to sell the poems.
13. See *The Collected Letters of Charlotte Smith*, ed. by Judith Phillips Stanton (Bloomington and Indianapolis: Indiana University Press, 2003).
14. See for instance George Cheyne, *The English Malady* (1737) and Robert James, *Medical Dictionary* (1743).
15. Janet Todd, *Sensibility: An Introduction* (London and New York: Methuen, 1986), 47.
16. See Vivien Jones, *Women in the Eighteenth Century: Constructions of Femininity* (London: Routledge, 1990), 85–6 for an extract from James's definition of hysteria.
17. Ibid. 86.
18. Sigmund Freud, 'Mourning and Melancholia', *The Standard Edition of the Complete Psychological Works of Sigmund Freud*, trans. and ed. by James Strachey (London: Hogarth, 1957), 244.
19. Judith Hawley, 'Charlotte Smith's *Elegiac Sonnets*: Losses and Gains', *Women's Poetry in the Enlightenment: The Making of a Canon, 1730–1820*, ed. by Isobel Armstrong and Virginia Blain (Basingstoke: Macmillan, 1999) 184–98.
20. Ibid. 195.
21. Freud, 'Mourning and Melancholia', 244.

22. The poem is one of three that refer to the death of Smith's daughter Anna Augusta (74, 78 and 82, although it is only a footnote to Sonnet 74 that draws attention to this). The earlier loss of two children, the first a son with no recorded name and the second eleven-year-old Benjamin Berney, had prompted Smith to write some of her earliest surviving poetry, the first few sonnets that she collected in the first edition of *Elegiac Sonnets*.
23. See Guinn Batten, *The Orphaned Imagination: Melancholy and Commodity Culture in English Romanticism* (Durham, NC: Duke University Press, 1998) for an account of the operation of melancholy in the work of Byron, Blake, Shelley and Wordsworth. Batten draws on the work of Julia Kristeva, Judith Butler and Slavoj Žižek who variously resist Oedipal models of loss and mourning as they are premised upon denial and repression.
24. *A Treasury of English Sonnets*, ed. by David M. Main (Manchester: Alexander Ireland and Co., 1880), 358.
25. Ibid. 359.

CHAPTER 2. GOSSIP AND POLITICS IN *DESMOND*

1. Smith translated Prévost's *Manon Lescaut*, published by Cadell in 1786. It was almost immediately withdrawn from sale because of one reader's disapproval of its moral tone and accusations of plagiarism.
2. Charlotte Smith, *Desmond, A Novel*, 3 vols (London: Robinson, 1972). References in this chapter are to *Desmond*, ed. by Antje Blank and Janet Todd (Ontario: Broadview Press, 2001), abbreviated to *D*.
3. References are to Edmund Burke, *Reflections on the Revolution in France and on the Proceedings in Certain Societies in London Relative to that Event*, ed. by Conor Cruise O'Brien ([1790]; Harmondsworth: Penguin, 1982).
4. Blakely Vermeule, 'Gossip and Literary Narrative', *Philosophy and Literature* 30:1 (2006), 102–17, p. 104. For another useful account of the status of gossip in literature see Patricia Ann Meyer Spacks, *Gossip* (New York: Knopf, 1985).
5. Burke, *Reflections*, 97.
6. Ibid. 127.
7. Mary Wollstonecraft, *A Vindication of the Rights of Men* (1790) in Sylvana Tomaselli (ed.), *A Vindication of the Rights of Men* and *A Vindication of the Rights of Woman* (Cambridge: Cambridge University Press, 1995), 7.
8. Desmond echoes Paine's rationalization of the French abolition of hereditary titles: 'The French constitution says, *There shall be no*

titles; and of consequence, all that class of equivocal generation, which in some countries is called *"aristocracy"*, and in others *"nobility"*, is done away, and the peer is exalted into MAN', Thomas Paine, *Rights of Man* ([1790]; Harmondsworth: Penguin, 1987), 80.

9. Alison Conway, 'Nationalism, Revolution, and the Female Body: Charlotte Smith's *Desmond*', *Women's Studies*, 24 (1995), 395–409, argues that there is a nationalist undercurrent in Desmond's relationships with Josephine and Geraldine. I have taken a slightly different line on the nationalist significance of Josephine and Geraldine's interchangeability in my reading of *Desmond* in *Women Writers and the English Nation in the 1790s: Romantic Belongings* (Cambridge: Cambridge University Press, 2000), 81–90.

10. Montfleuri suggests that de Boisbelle fell and Verney was wounded in the same attempt to drive French revolutionaries from Avignon (*D*, 411). Montfleuri's account of their fate is a corrective to that which he suspects Bethel has heard:

> Have you not heard in England, that Mr Verney, an English gentleman, travelling for his amusement, has been inhumanly fallen upon by a party of the national troops, and killed? – This is, I understand, the report that has universally gained credit: yet, I beg to assure you, that it was in attempting to drive the French from Avignon, which, in a fit of desperate valour, his party undertook; and not in any tumult, or even by the hands of ruffians, who are equally the dread and scourge of all parties, that Verney fell; and that, as I believe, Boisbelle has fallen also. (*D*, 412)

CHAPTER 3. DECLARATIONS OF INDEPENDENCE IN *THE OLD MANOR HOUSE*

1. Charlotte Smith, *The Old Manor House* (London: Joseph Bell, 1793). References in this chapter are to *The Old Manor House*, ed. by Jacqueline M. Labbe (Ontario: Broadview Press, 2002) abbreviated to *TOMH*.

2. The Broadview edition of *TOMH* includes extracts from notices and reviews of the novel. See *The Analytical Review*, 16 (May 1793), 60–3 and *The Critical Review*, 8 (May 1793), 44–54 for views on formal and moral deficiencies of the novel. *The Monthly Review*, 11 (May 1793), 150–3 was more generous, finding that 'it discovers, in a considerable degree, facility of invention, knowledge of life, and command of language' (*TOMH*, 531).

3. Joseph F. Bartolomeo, 'Subversion of Romance in *The Old Manor House*', *Studies in English Literature*, 33 (1993) 645–57, p.647. Bartolomeo responds in particular to Katherine M. Rogers, 'Inhibitions on Eighteenth-Century Women Novelists: Elizabeth

Inchbald and Charlotte Smith', *Eighteenth-Century Studies* 11:1 (Fall 1977), 63–78 and Mary Anne Schofield, *Masking and Unmasking the Female Mind: Disguising Romances in Feminine Fiction, 1713–1799* (Nebraska: University of Delaware Press, 1990).
4. Edmund Burke, *Reflections on the Revolution in France and on the Proceedings in Certain Societies in London Relative to that Event*, ed. by Conor Cruise O'Brien ([1790]; Harmondsworth: Penguin, 1982), 280. Burke also alludes to the French political constitution as a 'noble and venerable castle' (ibid. 121), whose walls have been torn down but whose foundations are intact.
5. Ibid. 140.
6. Jacqueline Labbe explores the issue of property rights and inheritance in her introductory essay to the Broadview edition of *TOMH*.
7. Burke, *Reflections*, 280. Burke also alludes to the French constitution as a 'noble and venerable castle' (ibid. 121).
8. Ibid. 280.
9. Ibid. 181.
10. Julia Kristeva, *Powers of Horror: An Essay on Abjection*, trans. by Leon Roudiez (New York: Columbia University Press, 1980).

CHAPTER 4. DOUBLE VISION AND THE *EMIGRANTS*

1. Letter to Joseph Cooper Walker, 20 February 1793, *The Collected Letters of Charlotte Smith*, ed. by Judith Phillips Stanton (Bloomington and Indianapolis: Indiana University Press, 2003), 62. Further references to this book are abbreviated to Stanton.
2. Charlotte Smith, *The Emigrants, a poem, in two books* (London: Cadell, 1793). References to the poem in this chapter are to *The Emigrants*, *The Poems of Charlotte Smith*, ed. by Stuart Curran (Oxford : Oxford University Press, 1993), 135–63, abbreviated to TE.
3. Cited in notes to Broadview edition of *Desmond*, 415.
4. More wrote a tract called *Remarks on the Speech of M. Dupont*, the proceeds of which were donated to the fund. The subject of the pamphlet was a speech by a member of the National Convention advocating the establishment of secular public schools in France.

CHAPTER 5. MOURNING COMPLETE?: *BEACHY HEAD*

1. *Beachy Head: with other poems and The Natural history of Birds, intended chiefly for young persons* (London: Joseph Johnson, 1807). References in this chapter are to *Beachy Head*, *The Poems of Charlotte Smith*, ed. by

Stuart Curran (New York: Oxford University Press, 1993), 213–47, abbreviated to *BH*.
2. See for instance Stanton, p.568, p. 694, p.696.
3. Theresa M. Kelley, 'Romantic Histories: Charlotte Smith and *Beachy Head*', *Nineteenth-Century Literature*, 59:3 (December 2004), 282–314, p.287.
4. Jacqueline Labbe makes a strong case that Smith's poetry anticipates many aspects of Wordsworth's poetry and that she should be regarded as one of the founding poets of Romanticism in *The Culture of Gender: Charlotte Smith, Poetry, and Romanticism* (Manchester: Manchester University Press, 2003).
5. Judith Pascoe explores Smith's interest in botany and considers women's relationship to the science in 'Female Botanists and the Poetry of Charlotte Smith', *Re-visioning Romanticism: British Women Writers 1776–1837*, ed. by Carol Shiner Wilson and Joel Haefner (Philadelphia: University of Pennsylvania Press, 1994), 193–209.
6. For instance, Theresa Kelly, 'Romantic Histories', Jacqueline Labbe *The Culture of Gender* and John M. Anderson 'Beachy Head: The Romantic Fragment poem as Mosaic', T*he Huntington Library Quarterly*, 63:4 (2000), 547–74 argue in various ways that the 'missing' epitaph is a self-conscious omission in the poem.
7. 'The delay which [has] taken place [in publishing the poem] has been occasioned partly by the hope of finding a preface to the present publication, which there was some reason to suppose herself had written' (*BH*, 215).
8. Wordsworth's note to 'Stanzas Suggested in a Steamboat off St Bees' Heads', *The Poetical Works of William Wordsworth* ed. by Ernest de Selincourt and Helen Darbishire, 5 vols (Oxford: Clarendon Press, 1949), vol. 4, 403.

CHAPTER 6. THE TIES THAT BIND: WILLIAMS' POETRY OF THE 1780s

1. Adam Smith, *Lectures on Rhetoric and Belles Lettres*, ed. by J.C.Bryce, *The Glasgow Edition of the Works and Correspondence of Adam Smith*, 6 vols (Oxford, 1983), vol. 4, 104.
2. Such accounts proceed from 'stadial' theories of social development, in which societies are understood to progress from one stage of organization to another, each stage more complex than the last (hunter-gatherer, pastoral, agricultural, commercial). For a helpful discussion of the relationship between such theories of historical development and historiography – the theory of history writing – in

the eighteenth century, see Karen O'Brien, *Narratives of Enlightenment: Cosmopolitan History from Voltaire to Gibbon* (Cambridge: Cambridge University Press, 1997).
3. Helen Maria Williams, *Poems, 1786*, 2 vols (Oxford: Woodstock Books, 1994), vol. 2, 53–4. References to this edition will be abbreviated to *Poems, 1786*.
4. For a discussion of cosmopolitanism and enlightenment historians, see O'Brien, *Narratives of Enlightenment*, 1–20.
5. Ibid. 9.
6. *Edwin and Eltruda, A Legendary Tale* (London: Cadell, 1782); references in this chapter are to *Edwin and Eltruda, A Legendary Tale* in *Poems, 1786*, 1, 61–100, abbreviated to *EE*.
7. *An American Tale*, in *Poems, 1786*, 1, 3–14. References are abbreviated to *AT*.
8. See Linda Colley, *Britons: Forging the Nation, 1707–1837* (New Haven: Yale University Press, 1992) for an account of the loyalist response to the American War.
9. William Robertson, *The History of America*, 3 vols (Dublin, 1777), vol. 1, p.v.
10. *An Ode on the Peace*, in *Poems, 1786*, 1, 35–60. References are abbreviated to *OP*. Williams published a second 'Ode on the Peace' in 1801, which was first published in the *Morning Chronicle* to mark the treaty signed by the English and the French that year.
11. A monody is an ode sung by a single voice in Greek tragedy or in this context a poem lamenting someone's death.
12. Anna Laetitia Barbauld, *Eighteen Hundred and Eleven: A Poem* (London: Johnson and Co., 1812), ll.313–16.
13. *Peru*, in *Poems, 1786*, 2, 45–178. References are to *Peru*.
14. See, for instance, *Eighteen Hundred and Eleven* and Percy Bysshe Shelley's 'Ode to Liberty' (1820), both visionary poems which respond to the burgeoning independence movements in South American colonies. Peru gained independence from Spain in 1824.
15. William Robertson, *The History of America*, 3 vols (Dublin, 1777), vol. 3, Bk. VI, 82.
16. *A Poem on the Bill Lately Passed for Regulating the Slave Trade* (London: Cadell, 1788). References are abbreviated to *RST*.

CHAPTER 7. PHILOSOPHICAL PASSION: *JULIA*

1. Helen Maria Williams, *Julia, A Novel*, 2 vols (London: Cadell, 1790). References to this edition are abbreviated to *Julia*.
2. See Gregory Dart, *Rousseau, Robespierre and English Romanticism* (Cambridge: Cambridge University Press, 1999) for an analysis of

the influence of Rousseau's philosophy on French Revolutionaries.
3. Eleanor Ty, *Unsex'd Revolutionaries: Five Women Novelists of the 1790s* (Toronto: University of Toronto Press, 1993), 81.
4. Mary Wollstonecraft may have revisited this vision of female communion in one of the projected endings of her unfinished novella, *Maria: or, The Wrongs of Woman*, in which the heroine, her daughter and her former warder turned confidante Jemima set up home together after Maria's lover proves unfaithful.
5. Ty, *Unsex'd Revolutionaries*, 76.
6. Ibid.
7. See Adela Pinch, *Strange Fits of Passion: Epistemologies of Emotion, Hume to Austen* (Stanford: Stanford University Press, 1996) for an excellent study of the way in which 'writers of the late eighteenth and early nineteenth centuries account for the relationships between persons and passions' (p.3).
8. Counter-revolutionaries of course reverse the analogy, depicting a 'frenzied' revolutionary reason driving out the benign force of sentimental attachment to King and country.
9. This is one of many poems of the late eighteenth century that anticipates Wordsworth's 'revolutionary' maxims in the Preface to the *Lyrical Ballads*, in particular here the idea that poetry is 'emotion recollected in tranquility'.
10. Mary Wollstonecraft, *A Vindication of the Rights of Woman* in *A Vindication of the Rights of Men with A Vindication of the Rights of Woman and Hints*, ed. by Sylvana Tomaselli (Cambridge: Cambridge University Press, 1995), 97.

CHAPTER 8. REVOLUTION AND ROMANCE: *LETTERS FROM FRANCE*

1. The *Letters* were published in two four-volume series (see Bibliography for details of individual titles). I shall refer to two different editions of the *Letters*. For Series One, Volume 1, I shall refer to *Letters Written in France, in the Summer 1790, to a Friend in England*, ed. by Neil Fraistat and Susan S. Lanser ([1790]; Ontario: Broadview Press, 2001). References are abbreviated to *LFF*, 1. For Series One, Volumes 2–4, and Series Two, Volumes 1–4 (which I have renumbered Volumes 2–8) I shall refer to *Letters From France*, ed. by Janet Todd, 8 vols (Delmar, New York: Scholars Facsimiles and Reprints, 1975). References are abbreviated to *LFF*, 2–8.
2. *The Analytical Review* (December 1790), 431.
3. *The Analytical; The Universal Magazine of Knowledge and Pleasure*

(December 1790), 289.
4. *The General Magazine* (December 1790), 541–43.
5. Ibid.
6. *The Gentleman's Magazine* (January 1791), 92–3.
7. See Mary Favret, 'Spectatrice as Spectacle: Helen Maria Williams At Home in the Revolution', *Studies in Romanticism*, 3:2 (Summer 1993), 273–95 for a fascinating discussion of the theatrical nature *of Letters From France*.
8. See Edmund Burke, *A Philosophical Enquiry into the Origin of Our Ideas of the Sublime and the Beautiful* (1757). See Steven Blakemore, *Crisis in Representation: Thomas Paine, Mary Wollstonecraft, Helen Maria Williams, and the Rewriting of the French Revolution* (Ontario and London: Associated University Presses, 1997) for more on Williams' reworking of Burke's *Enquiry*.
9. Jacqueline LeBlanc offers an important insight into Williams' enthusiasm for commercial and popular culture in France in 'Politics and Commercial Sensibility in Helen Maria Williams' *Letters from France*', *Eighteenth-Century Life*, 21:1 (February 1997), 26–44. See also my longer discussion of Williams' interest in commerce in the context of nationhood in *Women Writers and the English Nation in the 1790s: Romantic Belongings* (Cambridge: Cambridge University Press, 2000).
10. Warren Hastings, the Governor of Bengal, was on trial for mismanagement of his area of jurisdiction in Bengal from 1788 to 1795.
11. Mary Wollstonecraft, *An Historical and Moral View of the Origin and Progress of the French Revolution; and the Effect it has Produced in Europe* (1793).
12. See for instance Volume 7, and the description of a peasant woman from Arras led to the scaffold after nursing her baby: 'When she received the fatal stroke, the streams of nourishment issued rapidly from her bosom, and, mingled with her blood, bathed her executioner' (*LFF*, 7, 122).
13. The poem is reprinted in *LFF*, 1, 207–12. References are abbreviated to *FE*.
14. The French slave trade was abolished in 1793 and slavery in French colonies ended in 1794, though both were reinstated by Napoleon in 1802. The first bill to abolish the British slave trade was passed in 1807, though it was still legal to have slaves until 1833.
15. Laetitia Matilda Hawkins, *Letters on the Female Mind, Its Powers and Pursuits, Addressed to Miss H.M. Williams, With particular reference to her 'Letters' from France*, 2 vols (London: Hookham and Carpenter, 1793).
16. Ibid. 191.

NOTES

17. See Mary Favret, *Romantic Correspondence: Women, Politics and the Fiction of Letters* (Cambridge: Cambridge University Press, 1993) for a lengthy exploration of Williams' epistolary techniques and my discussion of her use of the letter as a sign of a receding public sphere in *Women Writers and the English Nation*.

CHAPTER 9. SUBLIME EXILE: *A TOUR IN SWITZERLAND*

1. Helen Maria Williams, *A Tour in Switzerland; or, A View of the Present State of the Governments and Manners of those Cantons; with Comparative Sketches of the Present State of Paris*, 2 vols (London: Robinson, 1798). References are abbreviated to *TS*.
2. These include: Charles Este, *A Journey in the Year 1793, through Flanders, Brabant and Germany to Switzerland* (London, 1795); Robert Gray, *Letters during the Course of a Tour through Germany, Switzerland and Italy in the Year M.DCC.XCV and M.DCC.XCII* (London, 1794); Rowley Lascelles, *Sketch of a Descriptive journey through Switzerland* (London, 1796).
3. Williams refers to the followers of Abraham Essendi and Theophilanthropy.
4. Nigel Leask, 'Salons, Alps and Cordilleras: Helen Maria Williams, Alexander von Humboldt, and the discourse of Romantic Travel' in Elizabeth Eger, Charlotte Grant, Cliona O'Gallchoir and Penny Warburton (eds.), *Women, Writing and the Public Sphere, 1700–1830* (Cambridge: Cambridge University Press, 2001), 217–39.
5. *The Monthly Review* (October 1798), 140.
6. *Poems on Various Subjects. With Introductory Remarks on the Present State of Science and Literature in France* (London: Whittaker, 1823), pp. xii–xiii. References are abbreviated to *Poems VS*.
7. *Researches concerning Inhabitants of America* (1814) and *Personal Narrative of Travels to . . . the New Continent* (1814).
8. *A Narrative of the Events Which Have Taken Place in France From the Landing of Napoleon Buonaparte to the Restoration of Louis XVIII* (1815); *Letters on the Events Which Have Passed in France Since the Restoration in 1815* (1819) and *On the Late Persecution of Protestants* (1816).

Select Bibliography

CHARLOTTE SMITH

Selected works

The Banished Man (London: Cadell and Davies, 1794).
Beachy Head, Fables, and Other Poems (London: Joseph Johnson, 1807).
Celestina. A novel (London: Cadell, 1791).
Conversations introducing Poetry... For the use of children and young persons (London: Joseph Johnson, 1804).
Desmond. A novel (London: Robinson, 1792).
Elegiac Sonnets and other Essays 'by Charlotte Smith of Bignor Park, Sussex' (London: Dodsley, 1784).
Elegiac Sonnets, vol. 2 (London: Cadell and Davies, 1797).
Emmeline, the Orphan of the Castle (London: Cadell, 1788).
Ethelinde, or the Recluse of the Lake (London: Cadell, 1789).
The Letters of a Solitary Wanderer, vols 1–3 (London: Sampson Low, 1800).
The Letters of a Solitary Wanderer, vols 4–5 (London: Longman, 1802).
Manon Lescaut, or, The Fatal Attachment, a translation of Abbé Prévost's *Manon L'Escaut* (London: Cadell 1785; withdrawn but published anonymously in 1786).
Marchmont. A novel (London: Sampson Low, 1796).
Minor Morals (London: Sampson Low, 1798).
Montalbert. A novel (London: Sampson Low, 1795).
The Natural history of Birds, intended chiefly for young persons (London: Joseph Johnson, 1807).
The Old Manor House. A Novel (London: Bell, 1793).
Rambles Farther. A Continuation of Rural Walks (London: Cadell and Davies, 1796).
The Romance of Real Life, a translation of stories in Gayot de Pivatol's *Les Causes Célèbres* (London: Cadell, 1787).
Rural Walks: in dialogues: intended for the use of young persons (London: Cadell and Davies, 1795).
The Wanderings of Warwick (London: Bell, 1794).

What Is She? A comedy in five acts (London: Longman, 1799).
The Young Philosopher. A Novel (Cadell and Davies, 1798).

Modern editions cited

The Collected Letters of Charlotte Smith ed. by Judith Phillips Stanton (Bloomington and Indianapolis: Indiana University Press, 2003). An invaluable collection and a turning-point for Charlotte Smith studies.

Desmond, ed. by Antje Blank and Janet Todd ([1792]; Ontario: Broadview, 2001).

The Old Manor House, ed. by Jaqueline M. Labbe ([1793]; Ontario: Broadview, 2002).

The Poems of Charlotte Smith, ed. by Stuart Curran (New York: Oxford University Press, 1993).

Biographies

Dorset, Catherine Ann, 'Charlotte Smith', in Sir Walter Scott, *Biographical Memoirs of Eminent Novelists* (Edinburgh, 1834). A sanitized account of Smith's politics and domestic life by her more conservative sister.

Hilbish, Florence May Anna, *Charlotte Smith, Poet and Novelist (1749–1806)* (Philadelphia: University of Pennsylvania Press, 1941). A pioneering study of the 'life in the works'.

Fletcher, Loraine, *Charlotte Smith: A Critical Biography* (Basingstoke: Palgrave, 1998). A 'Romantic' biography to the extent that it reads Smith's life in the works, albeit more self-consciously and with more nuance than Hilbish, to weave a compelling narrative with astute textual analysis.

Selected criticism

Bartolomeo, Joseph F., 'Subversion of Romance in *The Old Manor House*', *Studies in English Literature*, 33 (1993), 645–57. Bartolomeo contests earlier feminist critics of Smith who saw her trapped within the conservative conventions of romance.

———, 'Charlotte to Charles: The Old Manor House as a Source for *Great Expectations*', *Dickens Quarterly*, 8:3 (September 1991), 112–19.

Benis, Toby Ruth, '"A Likely Story": Charlotte Smith's Revolutionary Narratives' *European Romantic Review*, 14:3 (September 2003), 291–306. Benis considers the way in which Smith's novels share in the conversation of her contemporaries like Burke and Wordsworth about the impact of the French revolution on the form of narrative.

Brewer, William A., 'Charlotte Smith and the American Agrarian Ideal', *English Language Notes*, 40:4 (June 2003), 51–61.

Conway, Alison, 'Nationalism, Revolution, and the Female Body: Charlotte Smith's *Desmond*', *Women's Studies*, 24 (1995), 395–409. Conway's interesting and complex article draws parallels between the attempts of Mary Wollstonecraft and Smith to retrieve the female body from 'essentialist' politics and put it to use in revolutionary ways.

Crisafulli, Lilla Maria, 'Within or Without? Problems of Perspective in Charlotte Smith, Anna Laetitia Barbauld and Dorothy Wordsworth' in Lilla Maria Crisafulli and Cecilia Pietropoli (eds.) *Romantic Women Poets: Genre and Gender* (Amsterdam: Rodopi, 2007), 35–62. A rather curtailed consideration of Smith's Romantic, meditative subjectivity.

Curran, Stuart, 'Charlotte Smith and British Romanticism', Creating a Literary Series: The Brown University Women Writers Project and the Oxford University Press 'Women Writers in English, 1350–1850' Texts, *South Central Review*, 11:2 (Summer 1994), 66–78. Curran explains that Smith was the first woman writer to be included in the Oxford Women Writers series on the grounds of her contribution to the formal developments of Romanticism and by virtue of being possibly the first woman in the English-speaking world to live wholly on the proceeds of her writing.

Hawley, Judith, 'Charlotte Smith's *Elegiac Sonnets*: Losses and Gains', *Women's Poetry in the Enlightenment: The Making of a Canon, 1730–1820*, ed. by Isobel Armstrong and Virginia Blain (Basingstoke: Macmillan, 1999), 184–98. This is one of a number of pieces that tries to come to terms with the melancholic character of Smith's *Sonnets*.

Keane, Angela, *Women Writers and the English Nation in the 1790s: Romantic Belongings* (Cambridge: Cambridge University Press, 2000). My reading of Smith's fiction in this book foregrounds her complex engagement with English national identity, cosmopolitanism and French revolutionary nationalism.

Kelly, Theresa M., 'Romantic Histories: Charlotte Smith and *Beachy Head*', *Nineteenth-Century Literature*, 59:3 (2004), 281–314. A fascinating and densely argued study of the models of historical narrative Smith draws on in *Beachy Head*.

Kennedy, Deborah, 'Thorns and Roses: the Sonnets of Charlotte Smith', *Women's Writing*, 2:1 (1995), 43–53.

Labbe, Jacqueline M., 'Selling One's Sorrows: Charlotte Smith, Mary Robinson, and the Marketing of Poetry', *The Wordsworth Circle*, 25 (1994), 68–71.

———, 'Metaphoricity and the Romance of Property in *The Old Manor House*', *Novel: A Forum on Fiction*, 34:2 (Spring 2001), 216–31. Labbe's article foregrounds the status of property ownership in Smith's novel, arguing cogently that Smith calls into question the notion of ownership itself.

———, *The Culture of Gender: Charlotte Smith, Poetry, and Romanticism* (Manchester: Manchester University Press, 2003). Labbe astutely argues for the centrality of Smith's poetry to our understanding of Romanticism, in this eloquent, and impassioned, study.

Lokke, Kari E., 'The Mild Dominion of the Moon': Charlotte Smith and the Politics of Transcendence', *Rebellious Hearts: British Women Writers and the French Revolution*, ed. by Adriana Craciun and Kari E. Lokke (Albany, NY: SUNY Press), 85–106. Lokke argues against locating male and female Romantic poets on a binary of transcendence and immanence and finds in Smith's sonnets a poetics of feminine transcendence.

Miller, Judith Davis, 'The Politics of Truth and Deception: Charlotte Smith and the French Revolution', see Lokke, *Rebellious Hearts*, 337–63.

Pascoe, Judith, 'Female Botanists and the Poetry of Charlotte Smith', *Revisioning Romanticisim: British Women Writers, 1776–1837*, ed. by Carol Shiner Wilson and Joel Haefner (Philadelphia: University of Pennsylvania Press, 1994). Pascoe finds and contextualizes a scientific 'earth-bound' aesthetic in Smith's loco-descriptive poem *Beachy Head*, to counter the 'transcendent' aesthetic of Romanticism.

Richey, William, 'The Rhetoric of Sympathy in Smith and Wordsworth', *European Romantic Review*, 13 (2002), 427–43. Richey examines Smith's and Wordsworth's sonnets and humanitarian poems in the context of Adam Smith's ethics.

Rogers, Katherine M., 'Inhibitions on Eighteenth-Century Women Novelists: Elizabeth Inchbald and Charlotte Smith,' *Eighteenth-Century Studies*, 11:1 (Fall 1977), 63–78. One of the earlier pieces on Smith from late twentieth-century feminist critics who saw her fiction as trapped within patriarchal convention.

Schofield, Mary Anne, *Masking and Unmasking the Female Mind: Disguising Romances in Feminine Fiction, 1713–1799* (Nebraska: University of Delaware Press, 1990).

Stanton, Judith, 'Charlotte Smith and "Mr Monstroso": An Eighteenth-Century Marriage in Life and Fiction', *Women's Writing*, 7:1 (2000), 7–22. Stanton sketches a portrait of Smith's ill-fated marriage by raiding her edition of Smith's *Letters* and supplementing them with the fictionalized versions of her errant husband.

Tayebi, Kandi, 'Charlotte Smith and the quest for the romantic prophetic voice', *Women's Writing*, 11:3 (2004), 421–38. Tayebi considers Smith's writing as a rewriting of masculine poetic authority and the assertion of a new feminine poetics.

——, 'Undermining the Eighteenth-Century Pastoral: Rewriting the Poet's Relationship to Nature in Charlotte Smith's Poetry', *European Romantic Review*, 15:1 (March 2004), 131–50. Tayebi takes her cue from Stuart Curran and argues that Smith gives voice to the 'apparent contradictions in nature' to 'reveal and hopefully combat oppression'.

Ty, Eleanor, 'Revolutionary Politics: Domesticity and Monarchy in *Desmond*', in *Unsex'd Revolutionaries: Five Women Novelists of the 1790s* (Toronto: University of Toronto Press, 1993), 130–42.

Wheeler, Maxwell, 'Charlotte Smith's Historical Narratives and the English Subject', *Prism(s)*, 10 (2002), 7–18.

Wiley, Michael, 'The Geography of Displacement and Replacement in Charlotte Smith's *The Emigrants*', *European Romantic Review*, 17:1 (January 2006), 55–68. Wiley uses postmodern geography to argue that Smith reorganizes the dominant understanding of English and French spatial relations in *The Emigrants*.

Zimmerman, Sarah M., 'Varieties of Privacy in Charlotte Smith's Poetry', *European Romantic Review*, 18:4 (October 2007), 483–502. This is a substantial article in which Zimmerman insightfully interrogates the term 'private' in relation to Smith's *Elegiac Sonnets* and *Beachy Head*, finding in the former privacy as solitude and in the latter privacy as intimacy.

HELEN MARIA WILLIAMS

Selected works

The Charter, Lines Addressed by Helen Maria Williams, to her Nephew Athanase C.Coquerel, on His Wedding Day (Paris: 1819).

Edwin and Eltruda (London: Cadell, 1782).

A Farewell, for Two Years, to England (London: Cadell, 1791).

Julia, a Novel (London: Cadell, 1790).

Trans., *The Leper of the City of Aoste*, by Xavier de Maistre (London: George Cowie, 1817).

Letters from France, in the Summer of 1790, to a friend in England Containing Anecdotes Relative to the French Revolution and Memoirs of M. And Mme. Du F—, 5th edn. (London: Cadell, 1796), vol. 1.

Letters from France: Containing Many New Anecdotes Relative to the French Revolution, and the Present State of French Manners, 2nd edn. (London: Robinson, 1792), vol. 2.

Letters from France: Containing a Great Variety of Interesting and Original Information Concerning the Most Important Events which have Lately Occurred in that Country, and Particularly Respecting the Campaign of

1792, 2nd edn. (London: Robinson, 1796), vols. 3 an 4.

Letters Containing a Sketch of the Politics of France from the Thirty-first of May 1793, Till the Twenty-eighth of July 1794, and of the Scenes which Have Passed in the Prisons of Paris (London: Robinson, 1795), vols. 1 and 2.

Letters Containing a Sketch of the Scenes which Passed in Various Departments of France during the Tyranny of Robespierre; and of the Events which Took Place in Paris on the 28th July 1794 (London: Robinson, 1795), vol. 3.

Letters Containing a Sketch of the Politics of France, from the Twenty-eighth of July 1794, to the Establishment of the Constitution in 1795, and of the Scenes which have Passed in the Prisons of Paris (London: Robinson, 1796), vol. 4.

Letters on the Events Which have Passed in France Since the Restoration in 1815 (London: Baldwin, 1819).

'The Morai. An Ode', in Andrew Kippis, *The Life of Captain James Cook* (London: Robinson, 1788).

A Narrative of Events Which Have Taken Place in France from the Landing of Napoleon Bonaparte to the Restoration of Louis XVIII (London: Murray, 1815).

Ode on the Peace (London: Cadell, 1783).

'Ode to Peace', *Morning Chronicle* (17 November, 1801).

'On the death of the Rev. Dr. Kippis', *Gentleman's Magazine*, 66 (1796).

On the late Persecution of the Protestants (London: Underwood, 1816).

Trans. *Paul and Virginia*, by Bernadin de Saint-Pierre (London: Longman, 1795).

Trans. *Personal Narrative of Travels to the Equinoctial Regions of the New Continent, during the Years 1799–1804*, by Alexander von Humboldt (London: Longman, 1818–29).

Peru, A Poem. In Six Cantos (London: Cadell, 1784).

A Poem on the Bill Lately Passed for Regulating the Slave Trade (London: Cadell, 1788).

Poems, 2 vols. (London: Cadell, 1786).

Poems on Various Subjects (Whittaker: London 1823).

The Political and Confidential Correspondence of Lewis the Sixteenth, 3 vols (London: Robinson, 1803).

Trans., *Researches concerning the Institutions and Monuments of the Ancient Inhabitants of America, with Descriptions and Views of Some of the Most Striking Scenes in the Cordilleras!*, by Alexander von Humboldt (London: Longman, 1814).

Sketches of the State of Manners and Opinions in the French Republic (London: Robinson, 1801).

Souvenirs de la révolution française, trans. from English by Charles Coquerel (Paris: Doney-Dupré, 1827).

A Tour in Switzerland; or, A View of the Present State of the Governments and Manners of those Cantons: with Comparative Sketches of the Present State

of Paris, 2 vols. (London: Robinson, 1798).
Verses addressed by HMW to Her Two Nephews on Saint Helen's Day (Paris, 1809).

Modern editions cited

Letters From France, ed. by Janet Todd, 8 vols. (Delmar, New York: Scholars Facsimilies and Reprints, 1975).
Letters Written in France, in the Summer 1790, to a Friend in England, ed. by Neil Fraistat and Susan S. Lanser ([1790]; Ontario: Broadview Press, 2001).
Poems 1786, 2 vols, intro. by Jonathan Wordsworth (Oxford: Woodstock Facsimile, 1994).

Biographies

Kennedy, Deborah, *Helen Maria Williams and the Age of Revolution* (London: Associated University Presses, 2002). The first modern biography of Williams, it provides a comprehensive account of her life and sensitive readings of her texts. Kennedy draws on Williams' own memoir, *Souvenirs de la révolution française*, trans. by Charles Coquerel (Paris: Doney-Dupré, 1827).
Woodward, Lionel, *Une anglaise amie de la révolution française: Hélène-Maria Williams et ses amis* (Paris: Librarie Ancienne Honoré Champion, 1930).

Selected criticism

Adams, M. Ray, 'Helen Maria Williams and the French Revolution', *Wordsworth and Coleridge: Studies in Honor of George McLean Harper*, ed. by Earle Leslie Griggs (Princeton: Princeton University Press, 1939), 87–117. A rare, early twentieth-century, attempt to rescue Williams from ignominy, though Adams' portrait is not entirely flattering.
Blakemore, Steven, *Crisis in Representation: Thomas Paine, Mary Wollstonecraft, Helen Maria Williams and the Rewriting of the French Revolution* (Madison, Wisc.: Fairleigh Dickinson University Press, 1997). Blakemore situates Williams' *Letters* at the centre of the revolution debate.
———, 'Revolution and the French Disease: Laetitia Matilda Hawkins' *Letters to Helen Maria Williams*', *Studies in English Literature, 1500–1900*, 36:3 (Summer 1996), 673–691. A valuable contextualization of Hawkins's contemporaneous attack on Williams.
Favret, Mary, 'Spectatrice as Spectacle: Helen Maria Williams at Home

in the Revolution', *Studies in Romanticism*, 32:2 (July 1993), 273–95. Favret traces the spaces Williams inhabited during the revolution and reads them both literally and metaphorically in relation to women's place in the public sphere.

———, *Romantic Correspondence: Women, Politics and the Fiction of Letters* (Cambridge: Cambridge University Press, 1993). Favret's chapter on Williams' *Letters* is one of the first to attend to the form, as well as the content, of her *Letters*.

Guerra, Lia, 'Helen Maria Williams: The Shaping of a Poetic Identity', in Lilla Maria Crisafulli and Cecilia Pietropoli (eds.), *Romantic Women Poets: Genre and Gender* (Amsterdam: Rodopi, 2007), 63–76. Guerra speculates on the temporal gap between Williams' poetry publications.

Jones, Vivien, 'Women Writing Revolution: Narratives of History and Sexuality in Wollstonecraft and Williams', in *Beyond Romanticism: New Approaches to Texts and Contexts, 1780–1832*, ed. by Stephen Copley and John Whale, 1780-1832 (London: Routledge, 1992), 178–99. Jones addresses the novelistic paradigms employed by Williams in her *Letters* and Wollstonecraft's *Historical and Moral View*, finding both their radical potential and their ultimate failure to transform sexual ideology.

Keane, Angela, 'Helen Maria Williams' *Letters from France*: A National Romance', *Prose Studies* 15 (1992), 271–94. Here I foreground the romance tropes of Williams' *Letters*.

———, *Women Writers and the English Nation in the 1790s: Romantic Belongings* (Cambridge: Cambridge University Press, 2000). In the chapter on Williams, I address the *Letters* and Williams' negotiations with 'Englishness' throughout the 1790s.

Kelly, Gary, *Women, Writing and Revolution: 1790–1827* (Oxford: Clarendon Press, 1993).

Kennedy, Deborah, 'Benevolent Historian: Helen Maria Williams and Her British Readers', in Adriana Craciun and Kari E. Lokke (eds.), *Rebellious Hearts: British Women Writers and the French Revolution* (Albany, NY: SUNY, 2001), 317–36. Kennedy explores the *Letters* in the context of Williams' negotiations with the category of 'history', and traces the increasing hostility of her British reviewers.

Leask, Nigel, 'Salons, Alps and Cordilleras: Helen Maria Williams, Alexander von Humboldt, and the Discourse of Romantic Travel' in Elizabeth Eger, Charlotte Grant, Cliona O'Gallchoir and Penny Warburton (eds.), *Women, Writing and the Public Sphere, 1700–1830* (Cambridge: Cambridge University Press, 2001), 217–35. Leask considers Williams' *A Tour in Switzerland* and her translations of Humboldt's travels in South America and finds various intriguing sources of the sublime.

LeBlanc, Jacqueline, 'Politics and Commercial Sensibility in Helen Maria Williams' *Letters from France*', *Eighteenth-Century Life*, 21:1 (February 1997) 26–44. LeBlanc situates the *Letters* in the revolution debate, and illustrates the unusual marriage of political radicalism and commercial sensibility therein.

Ty, Eleanor, 'Resisting the Phallic: A Return to Maternal Values in *Julia*', in *Unsex'd Revolutionaries: Five Women Novelists of the 1790s* (Toronto: University of Toronto Press, 1993), 73–84. Ty's suggestive chapter on *Julia* reads the novel via Julia Kristeva's theory of the semiotic, and Chodorow and Gilligan's theories of the maternal ethos.

Index

Analytical Review, The 4, 32, 97, 99
André, John 77
Ariosto 40
Austen, Jane 67

Barbauld, Anna Laetitia 2, 79
   Eighteen Hundred and Eleven 78
Bartolomeo, Joseph 32–3
Bonaparte, Napoleon 119, 125, 128
Bowles, William Lisle 8
Brissot, Jacques Pierre 111
Brulart, Madame 105
Burke, Edmund 22, 23, 25, 44, 111, 128
   Enquiry into... the Sublime and the Beautiful 102
   Reflections on the Revolution in France 22, 34, 35, 43, 55, 106
Burney, Charles 44
Burney, Frances
   Evelina 21
Burns, Robert 13, 19
Byron, George Gordon 120

Cadell, Thomas 21
Canning, George
   'The New Morality' 4
Carbonnieres, Ramond de
   Observations on the Glacieres 122
Chatterton, Thomas 15
Cheyne, George,

The English Malady 16
Clarkson, Thomas 81
Coleridge, Samuel Taylor 8
Collier, Mary 13
Collins, William 15
Cooper Walker, Joseph 44, 58
Coquerel, Athanase 129, 130
Coquerel, Charles 129
Cowper, William 15, 44
   The Task 44
Coxe, William 121, 122, 123, 125
   Sketches of the... State of Switzerland 120
Critical Review, The 32
Curran, Stuart 8

Day, Thomas 81
Dauphin, Prince Louis 56
David, Jacques-Louis 114
Dickens, Charles 67
Dictionary of National Biography 5
Donne, John 8
Dryden, John 8
Duck, Stephen 13
Dyce 19

Earl of Egremont 67
European, The 75

Fletcher, Loraine 11, 18
Forbes, James 129
Freud, Sigmund
   'Mourning and Melancholia' 16–17

INDEX

du Fossé family 99, 107, 108, 111
Foucault, Michel 19

Gibbon, Edward 59, 119, 120
General Magazine, The 4, 100
Gentleman's Magazine, The 100
Godwin, William 4
Goldsmith, Oliver 13
  The Hermit 75
Goethe, Johann Wolfgang von
  The Sorrows of Young Werther
  11, 15, 21, 93
Gray, Thomas 20
  'Elegy...' 10, 11, 14, 53
Gregory, John
  Legacy to his Daughters 97

Hayley, William 67
Hawkins, Laetitia Matilda
  Letters on the Female Mind 4, 116,
  117
Hawley, Judith 17, 18
Holcroft, Thomas 4
Humboldt, Alexander von 129
Hume, David 58, 119

James, Robert
  Medical Dictionary 15
Johnson, Joseph 67
Johnson, Samuel 113

Kelly, Theresa 3, 59
Kennedy, Deborah 18
Kirkpatrick Sharpe, Charles
  'The Vision of Liberty' 4
Kristeva, Julia 41

Labbe, Jacqueline 10, 32–3
Las Casas, Bartolomé de 79–80
Leask, Nigel 125
Leblanc, Jacqueline 103
Linaeus 64
Louis XVI 55, 112
Lowes, Thomas 44

Macauley, Catherine 59, 70

Mackenzie, Henry 81
Mackintosh, James
  Vindicae Gallicae 22
Main, David M 18–19
Marie Antoinette 53, 106
Marx, Karl 59
Milton, John 8, 9, 54, 93
Mirabeau 110
Monthly Review, The 88, 128
More, Hannah 44, 81
Morning Chronicle, The 128

O'Brien, Karen 70

Paine, Thomas 4
  Rights of Man 22
Petrarch 8, 9
Polwhele, Richard
  The Unsex'd Females 2, 4
Pope, Alexander 8
Price, Richard 22, 23

Ramsay, David 74
Ramsay, James 81
Raynal, Guillaume Thomas 70, 74,
  79
Richardson, Samuel
  Clarissa 21, 88
  Sir Charles Grandison 21
Robespierre 46, 106, 109, 112,
  113, 114, 115, 119
Robertson, William 59, 70, 74, 79,
  119
Roscoe, William 81
Rousseau, Jean-Jacques 94, 120,
  121, 122, 124
  Julie, ou La Nouvelle Héloïse 21,
  88

Scott, Sarah 81
Scott, Walter 3
Seward, Anna
  'Monody on Major André' 77
Shakespeare, William 9
Shelley, Percy 79, 120
Sheridan, Frances

INDEX

The Memoirs of Miss Sidney Bidulph 21, 29–30, 88
Siddons, Sarah 102
Sidney, Sir Philip 9
Sillery, Madame, see Brulart
Smith, Adam 69
   The Wealth of Nations 83
Smith, Anna Augusta 44
Smith, Benjamin 7, 9, 67
Smith, Charlotte 130, 131
   The Banished Man 13, 44
   Beachy Head 5, 6, 59–60, 132
   Celestina 21
   Desmond 2, 21–31, 32, 33, 34, 89, 94
   Elegiac Sonnets 2, 7–20, 58, 59, 60, 93, 131
   The Emigrants 2, 5, 25–6, 33, 44–58, 59
   Emmeline 21
   Ethelinde 21
   The Old Manor House 26, 32–43, 72, 103
Sterne, Lawrence 81
   A Sentimental Journey 21
   Tristram Shandy 21
Stone, John Hurford 3, 117, 119, 130, 132
Swift, Jonathan 8

Todd, Janet 14, 15
Ty, Eleanor 87, 88

Vermeule, Blakey 23

Warren, Mercy Otis 70
Warton, Thomas,
   'The Pleasures of Melancholy' 15
Wilberforce, William 81
Williams, Cecilia 129
Williams, Helen Maria, 59, 131
   An American Tale 72, 74–6, 81, 84, 86
   'The Bastille' 129
   'The Charter' 130

Edwin and Eltruda 71–4, 81, 86
A Farewell, for Two Years, to England 109–10, 113
'A Hymn Written Among the Alps' 121
Letters From France 2, 3, 4, 5, 22, 24, 78, 84, 98, 99–118, 119, 126, 127, 128, 129, 130, 132
'An Ode on the Peace', 1783 76–8
'Ode on the Peace', 1801 128, 129
Peru 2, 69, 79–81, 84, 86
A Poem on the Bill...for Regulating the Slave Trade 81–4, 129
Julia 31, 72, 84, 85–98, 99, 101
Poems, 1786 6, 69–84, 128, 129
Poems on Various Subjects 128, 129
Sketches of the Manners and Opinions of the French Republic 128
Souvenirs de la révolution de la française 130
Tour in Switzerland 4, 114, 117, 119–28, 132
Williams, Persis 129
Wollstonecraft, Mary 105
   A Vindication of the Rights of Men 22
   A Vindication of the Rights of Woman 22, 23, 97
Wordsworth, Jonathan 70
Wordsworth, William 1, 6, 19, 20, 67–8, 120, 121
   and Samuel Taylor Coleridge, *Lyrical Ballads* 71
   sonnets 8
   Tintern Abbey 63

Yearsley, Ann 13
Young, Edward, 50
   Night Thoughts 10, 11, 14

www.ingramcontent.com/pod-product-compliance
Lightning Source LLC
Chambersburg PA
CBHW030139240426
43672CB00005B/193